SLOW COOKER SOUPS

SLOW COOKER SOUPS

A Cookbook of Comforting Recipes You Can Prep and Forget

Pamela Ellgen

ROCKRIDGE
PRESS

For general information on our other products and services or to obtain technical support, please contact our Customer Care Department within the U.S. at (866) 744-2665, or outside the U.S. at (510) 253-0500.

Rockridge Press publishes its books in a variety of electronic and print formats. Some content that appears in print may not be available in electronic books, and vice versa.

TRADEMARKS: Rockridge Press and the Rockridge Press logo are trademarks or registered trademarks of Callisto Media Inc. and/or its affiliates, in the United States and other countries, and may not be used without written permission. All other trademarks are the property of their respective owners. Rockridge Press is not associated with any product or vendor mentioned in this book.

Interior and Cover Designer: Rachel Haeseker
Art Manager: Samantha Ulban
Editor: Rebecca Markley
Production Editor: Ashley Polikoff
Photography © Laura Flippen, cover; Vera Lair/Stocksy, p. ii; Darren Muir, pp. vi, 20, 42; Ivan Solis, p. viii, Andrew Purcell, p. x, Hélène Dujardin, p. 12, Cameron Whitman/Stocksy, p. 24, Nataša Mandić/Stocksy, p. 44, StockFood / Bauer Syndication, pp. 60, 78, Cameron Whitman, p. 82, StockFood / News Life Media, p. 98, Trent Lanz / Stocksy, p.122. Author Photo Courtesy of © Rich Ellgen

ISBN: Print 978-1-64739-275-8 | eBook 978-1-64739-276-5

R0

for Rich

CONTENTS

Introduction ix

CHAPTER 1
The Slow-Cooking Soup Kitchen 1

CHAPTER 2
Stocks, Broths, and Clear Soups 13

CHAPTER 3
Pureed Soups 25

CHAPTER 4
Vegetable and Bean Soups 43

CHAPTER 5
Pasta and Grain Soups 61

CHAPTER 6
Chowders and Chilis 83

CHAPTER 7
Stews 99

Measurement Conversions 123
Resources 127
References 129
Index 130

INTRODUCTION

When I began writing this book, my primary motivation for cooking soups in a slow cooker was convenience. In addition to food writing, I worked full time at a health tech startup. Long hours and the intense nature of the job demanded my focus all day. By the time I got home, I just wanted to spend time with my kids or maybe sneak a surf session in. I didn't want to think about dinner. Many nights, that resulted in going out to eat. But the tab added up quickly!

As I neared the end of the first manuscript draft, a new motivation emerged. A global pandemic sent every sensible person into quarantine.
My job became even more demanding. I managed crisis communications from my home office while the kids bounced off the walls.

I needed to make healthy, frugal meals using pantry staples. Restaurants weren't an option. Neither was running to the fish market for the day's catch or to the farmers' market for seasonal vegetables. Even venturing out to the grocery store felt like taking my life in my hands or, worse, endangering someone else.

During this time, the kitchen became my sanctuary. The fragrance of onions, garlic, and ginger simmering in a rich coconut broth was especially comforting. When the world felt totally out of control, there was one thing I could do to make sense of it all: make soup.

So that's what I did. I cooked my way through bags of chickpeas and wild rice. I carefully rationed onions—although you wouldn't notice it from the recipes in this book—and garlic. And I rediscovered how much I could do with so little: even the simplest ingredients can become something magnificent when handled with care.

As it turned out, soup and a slow cooker answer many of life's challenges. They freed me up to tackle challenging problems at work. They fed my family and me through a really dark time. And they reminded me that good cooking doesn't have to use all of the latest gadgets or the most obscure ingredients.

A simple, slow-cooked soup is sometimes all you need.

CHAPTER 1

The Slow-Cooking Soup Kitchen

Before you jump straight into the recipes, here are a few essential pieces of equipment and some basic ingredients you'll need to get started. This chapter also has tips for salvaging soups gone wrong, storing and reheating soup, and navigating dietary restrictions.

Equipment

If you are into all the latest gadgets, that's cool. But you won't need them to make the recipes in this book. I'm a minimalist when it comes to cooking equipment.

Slow Cooker

Most of the recipes in this book can be made in a 6-quart slow cooker. Some will fit in a smaller crock. But I use the 6-quart size for nearly everything.

Chef's Knife

The only thing you really need to make the recipes in this book—other than a slow cooker, of course—is a good chef's knife. Buy the best one you can afford. It should have a sturdy handle and a stainless steel or ceramic blade and be kept sharp. A good chef's knife can last for years. I've had mine for nearly two decades, and it's still going strong.

Immersion Blender

For pureed soups, an immersion blender is more than helpful. It could spell the difference between a comforting meal and a chaotic soup explosion. When hot liquids are trapped in a regular blender, the heat can cause the steam to build pressure until it literally blows the lid off and sends scalding soup in all directions. If you don't have an immersion blender, puree the soup in a standard blender, but vent the lid and cover it with a kitchen towel.

Microplane Grater

A Microplane grater makes quick work of mincing garlic and ginger, zesting citrus fruits, and producing feathery shreds of parmesan that melt into your soup.

Wire-Mesh Strainer

For soups that involve straining out aromatics or bones, as in the case of chicken broth, a wire-mesh strainer is essential. I prefer a large strainer, roughly 6 inches across, with a handle and a lip on one side, so that it can be balanced over another dish for collecting the liquid.

Can Opener

Kind of obvious, but a can opener is essential for opening canned beans, tomatoes, and coconut milk.

The Great Broth Debate: Homemade or Store-Bought

Any chef will tell you that homemade broth or stock is best. Here's why: Homemade broth is fresh and free from preservatives. That alone has a tremendous effect on the flavor of the broth and your soup. When you make broth from scratch, you control every ingredient that goes into it. You can choose fresh, tasty, organic produce; carefully browned beef bones; and use the best salt when you make your own. Speaking of salt, store-bought broth often contains excessive amounts of sodium, so that your soup is oversalted before you even touch the salt cellar. Finally, making homemade broth is also a great way to reduce waste. When making soups and stews that call for bone-in meats, you can save the bones for stocks and other uses. They will keep in an airtight zip-top plastic bag in the refrigerator for up to 3 days or in the freezer for up to 3 months.

Nevertheless, you can't argue with the convenience of store-bought broth. Most of us don't really have the time to make two recipes—first the broth and then the soup. Fortunately, with the growing popularity of bone broth as a health food, artisan broths are increasingly available. Pick a broth that you wouldn't mind sipping from a spoon, and avoid bouillon cubes in all cases.

For me, a happy medium is making a large batch of broth and freezing it in 1-quart portions. Then I have the taste of homemade and the convenience of store-bought. Ultimately, never let time constraints stand in the way of making soup. Use what you have, and it will be good.

Ingredients

There are a handful of ingredients I use again and again in the recipes in this book. Have them on hand in your pantry or refrigerator so you can make a delicious soup whenever the urge strikes.

Prepared Broths and Stocks

Choose a brand whose taste you like, ideally with reduced sodium. Better than Bouillon makes excellent pastes that can be stirred into water to reconstitute.

Tomatoes and Tomato Paste

I use canned tomatoes and tomato paste in many of the recipes in this book. Whole plum tomatoes are a better choice than diced tomatoes. When making a recipe that calls for a small amount of tomato paste, buy a tube (it looks a little like a tube of toothpaste) instead of a small can, which may go bad before you can use it all.

Beans

Many of the recipes in this book call for beans. As much as I would love to call for dried beans, the slow cooker on low heat simply doesn't get hot enough to cook them properly—especially kidney beans. Canned beans are used in all cases. If you prefer to cook with dried beans, soak them in cool water overnight. Rinse and drain them, and then simmer them in fresh water on the stovetop until soft, 45 to 90 minutes, depending on the type of bean and its freshness. After this, they will be ready to use in the slow cooker.

Rice

A few different varieties of rice appear in this book, including wild rice, brown rice, and white rice. Store in covered containers or sealed plastic bags in your pantry. Rice will keep for months or even a year.

Onions

Yellow, red, and green onions are all used. The first two can be stored for weeks in a cool dark place. But be sure to keep them away from potatoes, which speed up spoilage. Wrap fresh green onions in a damp paper towel and then place in a plastic bag. They will keep in the refrigerator for about a week.

Carrots

Ideally, choose organic carrots. In many recipes, they are combined with onions and celery to serve as the flavor base called mirepoix.

Celery

Ideally, choose organic celery. Like carrots, celery is an essential component of mirepoix, which acts as a flavor base for many soups and stews.

Spices

A well-stocked spice rack will bring your soups to life. I usually have cumin, coriander, cinnamon, smoked paprika, red pepper flakes, turmeric, whole nutmeg, and curry powder on hand at any given time. Of course, freshly ground black pepper is a must.

Vinegars

I use red-wine vinegar, white-wine vinegar, balsamic vinegar, apple cider vinegar, and rice vinegar. But if you don't feel inclined to buy five bottles at a time, go for a good-quality white-wine vinegar. Make sure it doesn't have any other added ingredients, especially sugar.

Sea Salt or Kosher Salt

Whether you use sea salt or kosher salt, a good-quality, coarse salt is as important as your chef's knife. These salts have more flavor and less sodium (per teaspoon) than table salt. Don't even think about a low-sodium salt, though. It's not worth its salt.

Save Our Soup!

Uh-oh! What happens when your soup doesn't turn out how you expected? Before you pour it down the drain, here are a few options for salvaging it.

Too Salty

Pour out 1 cup of the soup liquid, and replace with 1 cup of water. If another liquid was used, such as milk, coconut milk, or broth, you can use that in addition to the water. However, don't add broth or stock that has salt.

Too Soft

Slow-cooking can sometimes produce vegetables that are more tender than you would like. Butternut squash or eggplant, for example, can sometimes end up in a state that's near mush. But don't fret; go all the way and puree the soup. If the soup contains pieces of meat, remove those first; then use an immersion blender to blend the soup until smooth.

Too Thin

For clear, broth-based soup, if the soup is too thin, pour some of the excess liquid out. For creamy soups, thoroughly whisk together 2 tablespoons of flour and 2 tablespoons of water. Add to the soup, and cook for another 5 minutes, or until thickened.

Too Bland

Salt may seem like the most obvious fix, but before you reach for the shaker, consider a couple other options. Add a few drops of red- or white-wine vinegar or lemon juice to the soup, tasting as you go. Roughly chop fresh herbs, such as cilantro, basil, parsley, or tarragon, and add them to the soup. Add a teaspoon of sugar or honey. For soups where it makes sense, add a teaspoon of adobo sauce or chili-garlic sauce to bring a little heat. Or, better yet, try multiple approaches until you reach a flavor that is perfectly robust and balanced.

Storing and Reheating

My primary motivation for using a slow cooker—and perhaps yours as well—is that with a little bit of effort, I can have a rich, delicious, and hot dinner waiting for me at the end of a long day. It's supposed to make life easier! In that spirit, each recipe in this book yields 6 to 8 portions. If you're going to go through the trouble of cooking it, you should get to enjoy it more than once. Here's how to get the most out of your leftovers.

Soup Storage

Pour leftover soup into a separate, heat-proof container. Transfer the container to the refrigerator until the soup is thoroughly chilled. A few stirs can help it cool down more quickly. Then cover with a tight-fitting lid. These might sound like a few extra steps, but they're for good reason. Food safety requires chilling food as quickly as possible. Storing the soup in the slow cooker crock would slow down this process. So too would covering the soup with a lid.

Store any garnishes, such as croutons, tortilla strips, salsa, nuts, yogurt, or parmesan, separately until you're ready to serve. Reheat the soup before garnishing.

Reheating Leftovers

You can reheat the soups in this book in the microwave, on the stovetop, or in the slow cooker. Only reheat the amount you intend to serve and eat at that time. The more often you heat and cool food, the higher the likelihood of allowing bacteria to flourish.

Microwave: Choose a microwave-safe container without a lid. Microwave the soup in 30-second intervals, stirring in between, until the soup is hot.

Stovetop: Pour the soup into a saucepan. Cover, and bring to a gentle simmer over medium heat. Cook for 2 to 4 minutes, stirring frequently, or until heated through. Remove from the heat, and serve.

Slow cooker: Slow-cook on high for 1 hour, or until hot. Or slow-cook for 2 hours on low heat, or until hot.

A Brief History of the Soup Kitchen

My first exposure to a soup kitchen was in Harlem. I was 19 and had never traveled far from the safety and comfort of suburbia on the opposite coast. One morning serving a few of New York's most vulnerable people was barely a token effort. But it opened my eyes to my privilege.

Throughout history, people have believed that sharing with those who are in need was a fundamental component of morality. The ancient Egyptians, for example, saw generosity as prerequisite to a blissful afterlife.

Several millennia later, when the Industrial Revolution disrupted traditional ways of life, poor people became poorer. Early social justice advocate Sir Benjamin Thompson wrote passionately about the need to provide for the hungry in the 1790s. His message took hold in London, where as many as 60,000 people relied on soup kitchens every day for their sustenance. But, by the 1830s, soup kitchens were banned in England for purportedly creating dependence and bringing vagrants.

Soup kitchens had a better trajectory in America years later. Hunger relief programs met the needs of immigrants following the Irish famine of the nineteenth century, and soup kitchens sprouted up around the country. The pressing need for soup kitchens increased again during the Great Depression and again in the early 1980s, an era of economic policies that failed to trickle down to the poorest in America.

Today, following the dramatic global increase in food prices in 2006, soup kitchens are more important than ever. Whether these kitchens are serving soup and bread or passing out diapers, the concept of the soup kitchen is an enduring and increasingly important way we care for one another.

About the Recipes

The whole point of a slow cooker is to make cooking mostly hands-off. Hence, the recipes in this book are designed for cooking low and slow all day. They can be prepared in about 10 minutes or less and then cook on low for 8 to 10 hours while you're at work. This concept pairs well with soup, which tends to taste best when it's had time to let the flavors develop.

I also created recipes that are accessible to anyone, including those with food allergies or dietary preferences. Recipes are labeled as follows, where appropriate:

- Dairy-Free

- Egg-Free

- Gluten-Free

- Nut-Free

- Vegan

- Vegetarian

As an added bonus, I've included several recipes for salads, croutons, and sandwiches that will pair well with the soups.

And please remember, for all recipes in this book that are labeled as allergen-free, always check ingredient packaging before purchasing in order to ensure they're truly free from the allergen.

Essential Vegetable Broth
page 14

CHAPTER 2

Stocks, Broths, and Clear Soups

Essential Vegetable Broth 14

Mushroom Stock 15

Kombu Dashi 16

Chicken Broth 17

Beef Stock 18

Fish Stock 19

Miso Soup 21

Wonton Broth 22

Essential Vegetable Broth

DAIRY-FREE • EGG-FREE • GLUTEN-FREE • NUT-FREE • VEGAN

Makes 1 gallon
Prep time: 5 minutes / Cook time: 8 to 10 hours

This broth serves as an excellent flavor base for any of the soups in this book. Instead of purchasing all of the ingredients to make this broth, I prefer to save vegetable scraps over time in the freezer, which can be taken straight from there to the slow cooker. Be conservative in salting the broth. An undersalted broth can correct an overly salty soup later on.

2 cups yellow
  onion pieces
1 cup carrot pieces
1 cup celery pieces
2 bell pepper cores,
  any color

Handful
  mushroom stems
4 fresh flat-leaf
  parsley sprigs
2 fresh thyme sprigs

1 teaspoon
  black peppercorns
½ teaspoon sea salt
1 gallon water

1. Put the onion, carrot, celery, bell pepper cores, mushroom stems, parsley, thyme, peppercorns, salt, and water in the slow cooker. Stir, then cover and cook on low for 8 to 10 hours.

2. Turn off the slow cooker. Strain the broth through a fine-mesh sieve. Discard the solids. Store the broth in a covered container in the refrigerator for up to 4 days or in the freezer for up to 3 months.

❋ **Substitution Tip:** If you're missing one of the ingredients, don't worry, just skip it.

Per Serving (1 cup): Calories: 13; Total Fat: 0g; Saturated Fat: 0g; Carbohydrates: 3g; Sodium: 73mg; Fiber: 0g; Protein: 0g

Mushroom Stock

Makes 1 gallon
Prep time: 5 minutes / Cook time: 8 to 10 hours

This hearty stock is a great stand-in for beef broth when making vegetarian recipes because of the savory umami flavors in the mushrooms. Use it in cream of mushroom soup, wild rice stews, and even risotto.

1 pound fresh
  mushrooms, rinsed
  and quartered
1 yellow onion, halved
1 small carrot,
  coarsely chopped

1 celery stalk,
  coarsely chopped
1 ounce
  dried mushrooms
2 fresh thyme sprigs

½ teaspoon
  black peppercorns
½ teaspoon sea salt
1 gallon water

1. Put the fresh mushrooms, onion, carrot, celery, dried mushrooms, thyme, peppercorns, salt, and water in the slow cooker. Stir, then cover and cook on low for 8 to 10 hours.

2. Turn off the slow cooker. Strain the stock through a fine-mesh sieve. Discard the solids. Store the stock in a covered container in the refrigerator for up to 4 days or in the freezer for up to 3 months.

   Flavor Tip: If you observe any grit in the broth from the mushrooms, pour the stock through a clean coffee filter or nut milk bag to remove.

Per Serving (1 cup): Calories: 15; Total Fat: 0g; Saturated Fat: 0g; Carbohydrates: 3g; Sodium: 73mg; Fiber: 0g; Protein: 0g

Kombu Dashi

DAIRY-FREE ● EGG-FREE ● GLUTEN-FREE ● NUT-FREE ● VEGAN

Makes 8 cups
Prep time: 5 minutes / Cook time: 1 hour

This broth is the vegan equivalent of fish stock. Kombu is dried sea kelp and has a flavor faintly reminiscent of the sea with a subtle minerality and saltiness. It can be found in your supermarket with the Japanese specialty items or ordered online. The broth is a delicious base for Japanese soups and seafood stews. It has a short cook time, which should not exceed 1 hour, as that will alter the flavor.

2 (4- to 6-inch) square pieces kombu

8 cups water

1. Put the kombu and water in the slow cooker. Stir, then cover and cook on low for 1 hour.

2. Turn off the slow cooker. Remove the kombu and discard. Store the broth in a covered container in the refrigerator for up to 3 days.

＊ **Flavor Tip:** For a little more umami flavor, add a handful of dried shiitake mushrooms.

Per Serving (1 cup): Calories: 1; Total Fat: 0g; Saturated Fat: 0g; Carbohydrates: 0g; Sodium: 30mg; Fiber: 0g; Protein: 0g

Chicken Broth

Makes 1 gallon
Prep time: 5 minutes / Cook time: 8 to 10 hours

This recipe yields not only a rich, flavorful broth but also a few cups of cooked chicken. I like to make a large batch and store it in the freezer for use later. In addition to its obvious use in soups, it makes for an excellent base for cooking vegetables or stirring into risotto.

4 bone-in chicken thighs, skinned

1 yellow onion, quartered

1 celery stalk, coarsely chopped

1 carrot, coarsely chopped

1 garlic clove, smashed

1 teaspoon black peppercorns

2 fresh thyme sprigs

½ teaspoon sea salt

1 gallon water

1. Put the chicken, onion, celery, carrot, garlic, peppercorns, thyme, salt, and water in the slow cooker. Stir, then cover and cook on low for 8 to 10 hours.

2. Turn off the slow cooker. Strain the broth through a fine-mesh sieve. Discard the solids. Remove the chicken meat from the bone, and reserve for another use. Store the broth in a covered container in the refrigerator for up to 5 days or in the freezer for up to 3 months.

Substitution Tip: If you have leftover chicken bones, from a roasted chicken, for example, use those in place of the chicken thighs. The flavor will be almost identical.

Per Serving (1 cup): Calories: 21; Total Fat: 1g; Saturated Fat: 0g; Carbohydrates: 1g; Sodium: 73mg; Fiber: 0g; Protein: 2g

Beef Stock

DAIRY-FREE • EGG-FREE • GLUTEN-FREE • NUT-FREE

Makes 1 gallon
Prep time: 5 minutes / Cook time: 8 to 10 hours, plus 45 minutes roasting time

Although beef stock requires a few additional steps to make, the results are worth the extra effort. Unlike browning chicken meat and bones, roasting beef bones isn't optional. If you don't do it, the stock will have a metallic taste. It's still a pretty hands-off process, though.

2 pounds beef bones
1 carrot, halved
½ yellow onion
1 tablespoon canola oil

1 celery stalk, halved
1 teaspoon black
   peppercorns

½ teaspoon sea salt
1 gallon water

1. Preheat the oven to 375°F.
2. On a rimmed baking sheet, coat the beef bones, carrot, and onion in the oil. Spread them out in an even layer.
3. Transfer the baking sheet to the oven. Roast for 35 to 45 minutes, turning the bones occasionally. (Do not let them burn.) Remove from the oven.
4. Transfer the roasted bones, carrot, and onion to the slow cooker.
5. Add the celery, peppercorns, salt, and water. Stir, then cover and cook on low for 8 to 10 hours.
6. Turn off the slow cooker. Strain the stock through a fine-mesh sieve. Discard the vegetables. Store the stock in a covered container in the refrigerator for up to 4 days or in the freezer for up to 3 months.

   Time-Saving Prep Tip: To save time, roast the bones, carrot, and onion ahead of time. Allow them to cool completely and then transfer to a zip-top plastic bag. Remove as much air as possible from the bag, and store in the refrigerator for 2 to 3 days or in the freezer for 1 to 2 months.

Per Serving (1 cup): Calories: 12; Total Fat: 0g; Saturated Fat: 0g; Carbohydrates: 1g; Sodium: 73mg; Fiber: 0g; Protein: 2g

Fish Stock

DAIRY-FREE • EGG-FREE • GLUTEN-FREE • NUT-FREE

Makes 1 gallon
Prep time: 5 minutes / Cook time: 3 hours

The subtlety of this stock works beautifully in seafood stews. It has a pleasant seawater aroma and a flavor that doesn't overpower other ingredients the way chicken broth or vegetable broth might. Ask your fishmonger to save unused fish pieces for you instead of purchasing a whole fish. Alternately, purchase a whole fish and fillet it yourself, using the head, bones, and tail to make the stock.

1 pound fish pieces, such as head, tail, and bones
1 shallot, halved
1 celery stalk, halved

1 garlic clove, smashed
2 fresh parsley sprigs
½ cup dry white wine
1 gallon water

½ teaspoon black peppercorns
½ teaspoon sea salt

1. Put the fish, shallot, celery, garlic, parsley, white wine, water, peppercorns, and salt in the slow cooker. Stir, then cover and cook on low for 3 hours.

2. Turn off the slow cooker. Strain the stock through a fine-mesh sieve. Discard the solids. Store the stock in a covered container in the refrigerator for up to 3 days or in the freezer for up to 2 months.

Flavor Tip: Be very careful not to let this stock come to a boil. It will bring out unpleasant flavors in the fish. Most of the time that is not a problem when slow-cooking, especially on low heat.

Per Serving (1 cup): Calories: 40; Total Fat: 2g; Saturated Fat: 0g; Carbohydrates: 0g; Sodium: 109mg; Fiber: 0g; Protein: 5g

Miso Soup

DAIRY-FREE • EGG-FREE • GLUTEN-FREE • NUT-FREE • VEGAN

Serves 4

Prep time: 5 minutes / Cook time: 2 to 3 hours

I have grown to love the flavor of miso. When you purchase miso paste instead of buying miso soup, the flavor is remarkably different. It has a pleasant saltiness and surprising sweetness. These flavors permeate this simple soup.

8 cups Kombu Dashi (page 16)
¼ cup white miso
8 ounces silken tofu, diced

2 scallions, white and green parts, thinly sliced

Freshly ground black pepper

1. Put the dashi and miso in the slow cooker. Whisk gently to dissolve the miso.
2. Add the tofu. Stir, then cover and cook on low for 2 to 3 hours.
3. Turn off the slow cooker. Add the scallions, and stir. Divide the soup among serving bowls and add pepper.

Tip: The white miso products I have seen are nearly all gluten-free, since they are made with rice. However, always read the label if you follow a gluten-free diet.

Per Serving: Calories: 71; Total Fat: 3g; Saturated Fat: 1g; Carbohydrates: 6g; Sodium: 647mg; Fiber: 1g; Protein: 6g

Wonton Broth

Serves 4

Prep time: 5 minutes / Cook time: 4 hours

This simple soup is a comforting, lighter alternative to chicken noodle soup when you're feeling a little under the weather. It also makes for a perfect backdrop for a savory, rich wonton soup.

2 garlic cloves, smashed

1 (1-inch) piece fresh ginger, halved

1 ounce dried shiitake mushrooms

2 tablespoons white miso

8 cups Chicken Broth (page 17) or store-bought

2 scallions, white and green parts, thinly sliced

2 heads baby bok choy, shredded

1. Put the garlic, ginger, dried mushrooms, miso, and broth in the slow cooker. Stir, then cover and cook on low for 4 hours.

2. Turn off the slow cooker. Strain the broth, and discard the solids.

3. Stir in the scallions and bok choy. Let the soup rest for about 2 minutes, then divide among serving bowls.

Flavor Tip: To bring out the most flavor in the ginger, place each half on a cutting board. Use the broad side of a knife to gently crush the ginger. It should remain intact but have far more surface area to release its delicious flavors.

Per Serving: Calories: 57; Total Fat: 1g; Saturated Fat: 0g; Carbohydrates: 12g; Sodium: 73mg; Fiber: 2g; Protein: 3g

Tomato Soup with Sourdough Asiago Grilled Cheese
pages 26–27

CHAPTER 3

Pureed Soups

Tomato Soup 26

   BONUS: Sourdough Asiago Grilled Cheese 27

Sweet Potato and Carrot Soup 28

   BONUS: Dukkah 29

Roasted Red Pepper Soup 30

Creamy Parsnip Bisque 31

Hearty Cream of Mushroom Soup 32

Thai Red Lentil Soup 33

Creamy Cauliflower Bisque 34

   BONUS: Herbed Bread Crumbs 35

Cream of Broccoli Soup 36

Potato-Leek Soup 37

Cannellini Bean and Cheddar Bisque 38

Tortilla Soup 39

Spinach and Apple Soup with Crumbled Bacon 40

Tomato Soup

DAIRY-FREE ● EGG-FREE ● GLUTEN-FREE ● NUT-FREE ● VEGAN

Serves 6

Prep time: 10 minutes / Cook time: 8 to 10 hours

Is there anything more comforting than tomato soup? Yes, there is: tomato soup from scratch that has simmered all day with virtually no effort. For a complete meal, serve with the Sourdough Asiago Grilled Cheese (recipe follows).

1 cup diced yellow onion

¼ cup extra-virgin olive oil, plus more for serving

4 garlic cloves, smashed

¼ cup tomato paste

1 cup coarsely chopped fresh basil, divided

½ teaspoon sea salt

2 (28-ounce) cans whole plum tomatoes

4 fresh thyme sprigs, plus more for serving

4 cups Essential Vegetable Broth (page 14) or store-bought

1. Put the onion, oil, garlic, tomato paste, all but 2 tablespoons of basil, the salt, tomatoes, thyme, and broth in the slow cooker. Stir, then cover and cook on low for 8 to 10 hours.

2. Turn off the slow cooker. Remove the thyme sprigs. Using an immersion blender, puree the soup until smooth. Divide among serving bowls.

3. Sprinkle some of the remaining 2 tablespoons of basil or the thyme over each serving for garnish. Drizzle with olive oil.

❋ **Flavor Tip:** To make the soup creamy, add ½ cup heavy cream in step 2, just before blending.

Per Serving: Calories: 145; Total Fat: 10g; Saturated Fat: 1g; Carbohydrates: 15g; Sodium: 506mg; Fiber: 6g; Protein: 3g

Sourdough Asiago Grilled Cheese

EGG-FREE • NUT-FREE • VEGETARIAN

Serves 2

Prep time: 5 minutes / Cook time: 6 to 8 minutes

2 tablespoons butter, at room temperature

4 sourdough bread slices

4 (¼-inch-thick) Asiago cheese or mozzarella cheese slices

1. Heat a large skillet over medium heat.
2. Butter one side of each slice of bread. Sandwich the cheese slices between the non-buttered sides of the slices.
3. Put the sandwiches in the skillet, and cook for 3 to 4 minutes on each of the buttered sides, or until golden brown. Remove from the heat.

Per Serving: Calories: 446; Total Fat: 26g; Saturated Fat: 15g; Carbohydrates: 34g; Sodium: 832mg; Fiber: 1g; Protein: 20g

Sweet Potato and Carrot Soup

EGG-FREE • GLUTEN-FREE • VEGETARIAN

Serves 6

Prep time: 10 minutes / Cook time: 8 to 10 hours

The sweet root vegetables in this recipe blend beautifully, making a silky-smooth soup with subtle spice. Crunchy dukkah—a Middle Eastern condiment made of nuts, seeds, and spices—and tangy yogurt provide contrast in texture and flavor. If you want a little more substance, serve the soup over steamed brown jasmine rice.

1 pound sweet potatoes, peeled and diced

1 pound carrots, diced

¼ teaspoon ground coriander

¼ teaspoon red pepper flakes

½ teaspoon sea salt, plus more as needed

8 cups Essential Vegetable Broth (page 14) or store-bought

Freshly ground black pepper

1 cup full-fat plain yogurt, for serving

½ cup Dukkah (recipe follows), for serving

1. Put the sweet potatoes, carrots, coriander, red pepper flakes, salt, and broth in the slow cooker. Stir, then cover and cook on low for 8 to 10 hours.

2. Turn off the slow cooker. Using an immersion blender, puree the soup until smooth. Taste and adjust the seasoning, if needed. Divide among serving bowls.

3. On each serving, dollop a generous 2 tablespoons of yogurt, and sprinkle 1 heaping tablespoon of dukkah.

✳ **Variation Tip:** For a vegan version, use a plain coconut or cashew milk yogurt.

Per Serving: Calories: 121; Total Fat: 2g; Saturated Fat: 1g; Carbohydrates: 24g; Sodium: 400mg; Fiber: 4g; Protein: 3g

Dukkah

Makes 1 cup
Prep time: 5 minutes

2 tablespoons coriander seeds, toasted

2 tablespoons black peppercorns
½ cup roasted pistachios

¼ cup sesame seeds
1 teaspoon coarse sea salt

1. Using a mortar and pestle, clean coffee grinder, or spice grinder, coarsely grind the coriander and peppercorns. Transfer to a food processor.

2. Add the pistachios, and pulse a few times, until coarsely ground.

3. Stir in the sesame seeds and salt. Store in a covered container for up to 1 month.

Per Serving (1 tablespoon): Calories: 39; Total Fat: 3g; Saturated Fat: 0g; Carbohydrates: 2g; Sodium: 147mg; Fiber: 1g; Protein: 1g

Roasted Red Pepper Soup

DAIRY-FREE ● EGG-FREE ● GLUTEN-FREE ● NUT-FREE ● VEGAN

Serves 6

Prep time: 5 minutes / Cook time: 8 to 10 hours

Creamy, smoky, and delicious, this blended soup is reminiscent of romesco sauce. Unlike the Spanish sauce, this soup contains no almonds or bread. Make sure not to add the vinegar until the end, so that it retains its bright acidity. If you have extra soup, it makes an excellent pasta sauce.

2 (11-ounce) jars roasted red peppers, drained

1 (15-ounce) can whole or diced plum tomatoes, drained

4 garlic cloves, smashed

¼ cup extra-virgin olive oil

1 tablespoon smoked paprika

½ teaspoon sea salt, plus more as needed

¼ teaspoon cayenne

4 cups Essential Vegetable Broth (page 14) or store-bought

1 tablespoon sherry vinegar or apple cider vinegar

Freshly ground black pepper

1. Put the peppers, tomatoes, garlic, oil, paprika, salt, cayenne, and broth in the slow cooker. Stir, then cover and cook on low for 8 to 10 hours.

2. Turn off the slow cooker. Stir in the vinegar. Using an immersion blender, puree the soup until smooth. Taste and adjust the seasoning, if needed. Divide among serving bowls.

Flavor Tip: For the best flavor, choose jarred piquillo peppers.

Per Serving: Calories: 125; Total Fat: 10g; Saturated Fat: 1g; Carbohydrates: 10g; Sodium: 584mg; Fiber: 3g; Protein: 2g

Creamy Parsnip Bisque

EGG-FREE ○ GLUTEN-FREE ○ VEGETARIAN

Serves 6

Prep time: 10 minutes / Cook time: 8 to 10 hours

Yukon gold potatoes give this creamy parsnip bisque a little more starch for a decadent texture and to balance the peppery flavor of the parsnips.

1 pound Yukon gold potatoes, peeled and diced

1 pound parsnips, peeled and diced

½ teaspoon sea salt, plus more as needed

1 teaspoon fresh thyme leaves

8 cups Essential Vegetable Broth (page 14) or store-bought

1 cup full-fat plain yogurt, for serving

Freshly ground black pepper

1. Put the potatoes, parsnips, salt, thyme leaves, and broth in the slow cooker. Stir, then cover and cook on low for 8 to 10 hours.

2. Turn off the slow cooker. Add the yogurt. Using an immersion blender, puree the soup until smooth. Add pepper. Taste and adjust the seasoning, if needed. Divide among serving bowls.

※ **Variation Tip:** For a thicker parsnip puree—the kind of thing you would serve on a plate underneath roasted chicken—omit all but 2 cups of broth. Cook as directed, and puree until silky smooth.

Per Serving: Calories: 189; Total Fat: 5g; Saturated Fat: 1g; Carbohydrates: 53g; Sodium: 133mg; Fiber: 6g; Protein: 9g

Hearty Cream of Mushroom Soup

EGG-FREE • GLUTEN-FREE • NUT-FREE • VEGETARIAN

Serves 6

Prep time: 5 minutes / Cook time: 8 to 10 hours

Do you know what the original plant-based meat substitute is? Mushrooms. Here's why: The glutamic acids in mushrooms generate a similar umami flavor to meat. This soup has fresh cremini mushrooms, fresh wild mushrooms, and a mushroom broth for a savory, bold flavor.

1 pound cremini mushrooms, sliced

1 yellow onion, diced

4 garlic cloves, smashed

¼ cup dry white wine or 2 teaspoons white-wine vinegar

¼ cup short-grain white rice

1 ounce dried wild mushrooms

1 teaspoon minced fresh thyme

8 cups Mushroom Stock (page 15) or store-bought vegetable broth

½ cup heavy cream

Sea salt

Freshly ground black pepper

1. Put the cremini mushrooms, onion, garlic, wine, rice, wild mushrooms, thyme, and stock in the slow cooker. Stir, then cover and cook on low for 8 to 10 hours.

2. Turn off the slow cooker. Using a small fine-mesh sieve, scoop out about ½ cup of mushrooms, and reserve.

3. Pour in the heavy cream. Using an immersion blender, puree the soup until smooth. Taste and adjust the seasoning, if needed.

4. Stir in the reserved mushrooms. Divide the soup among serving bowls.

 * **Flavor Tip:** To really amp up the mushroom flavor, spend an additional 10 minutes browning them in a pan with a few tablespoons of butter. Do this in batches (you made need to add a little bit more butter with each batch).

 * **Substitution Tip:** If you don't have homemade mushroom stock on hand (or don't have time to make it), I prefer to replace it with store-bought chicken broth. But use store-bought vegetable broth if you want to keep the soup vegetarian.

Per Serving: Calories: 143; Total Fat: 8g; Saturated Fat: 5g; Carbohydrates: 15g; Sodium: 156mg; Fiber: 3g; Protein: 3g

Thai Red Lentil Soup

DAIRY-FREE • EGG-FREE • GLUTEN-FREE • VEGAN

Serves 6

Prep time: 5 minutes / Cook time: 8 to 10 hours

Fragrant red curry paste, ginger, and garlic permeate hearty red lentils in this nourishing soup. Although this soup's roots are in Thai cooking, I have honestly never seen lentils in any Thai restaurant or cookbook. But they do lend body and color to this healthy, plant-based soup that's bursting with flavor. If you don't need the soup to be vegetarian, a splash of fish sauce will give it added depth.

1½ cups red lentils
1 yellow onion, diced
4 garlic cloves, diced
2 tablespoons red
  curry paste
1 tablespoon minced
  fresh ginger

½ teaspoon sea salt, plus
  more as needed
¼ teaspoon red
  pepper flakes
2 (15-ounce) cans
  full-fat coconut milk

8 cups Essential
  Vegetable
  Broth (page 14)
  or store-bought
Juice of 1 lime
Freshly ground
  black pepper

1. Put the lentils, onion, garlic, curry paste, ginger, salt, red pepper flakes, coconut milk, and broth in the slow cooker. Stir, then cover and cook on low for 8 to 10 hours.

2. Turn off the slow cooker. Stir in the lime juice. Using an immersion blender, puree the soup until smooth. Taste and adjust the seasoning, if needed. Divide among serving bowls.

   Variation Tip: For a green curry, opt for green lentils and green curry paste. If you can get your hands on some fresh makrut lime leaves, they will really amp up the flavor.

Per Serving: Calories: 471; Total Fat: 32g; Saturated Fat: 27g; Carbohydrates: 39g; Sodium: 318mg; Fiber: 7g; Protein: 15g

Creamy Cauliflower Bisque

EGG-FREE • GLUTEN-FREE • NUT-FREE

Serves 6

Prep time: 10 minutes / Cook time: 8 to 10 hours

Of all the cruciferous vegetables, cauliflower has the most subtle flavor. It can easily disappear behind bolder ingredients, such as pungent garlic or pecorino cheese. In this soup, the ingredients are well balanced to provide a rich and velvety puree. To keep the soup a uniform color, use herb sprigs, which can be removed, instead of adding minced herbs. If desired, top with Herbed Bread Crumbs (recipe follows).

1 head cauliflower, trimmed and coarsely chopped
1 Russet potato, peeled and coarsely chopped
1 cup diced yellow onion
4 garlic cloves, smashed

2 fresh thyme sprigs
2 fresh flat-leaf parsley sprigs
8 cups Chicken Broth (page 17) or store-bought
½ cup heavy cream

½ cup grated pecorino cheese
Sea salt
Freshly ground black pepper

1. Put the cauliflower, potato, onion, garlic, thyme, parsley, and broth in the slow cooker. Stir, then cover and cook on low for 8 to 10 hours.

2. Turn off the slow cooker. Remove the thyme and parsley.

3. Add the heavy cream. Using an immersion blender, puree the soup until smooth.

4. Stir in the cheese. Taste and adjust the seasoning, if needed. Divide the soup among serving bowls.

* **Flavor Tip:** Pecorino is a fairly salty cheese, so be careful about adding salt to the soup until you taste it.

Per Serving: Calories: 201; Total Fat: 10g; Saturated Fat: 6g; Carbohydrates: 23g; Sodium: 304mg; Fiber: 4g; Protein: 7g

Herbed Bread Crumbs

DAIRY-FREE • EGG-FREE • VEGAN

Makes 2 cups
Prep time: 5 minutes / Cook time: 5 to 7 minutes

2 tablespoons pine nuts, toasted

2 cups cubed French bread, crusts removed

1 teaspoon minced fresh thyme

1 teaspoon minced fresh rosemary

¼ teaspoon sea salt

2 tablespoons extra-virgin olive oil

1. Preheat the oven to 350°F.
2. Put the pine nuts in a food processor, and pulse until coarsely ground.
3. Add the bread, thyme, rosemary, and salt. Pulse until the bread has become fine crumbs.
4. Drizzle in the oil, and pulse once or twice just to integrate.
5. On a rimmed baking sheet, spread out the crumb mixture.
6. Transfer the baking sheet to the oven, and toast for 5 to 7 minutes, stirring once or twice. Be careful not to burn. Remove from the oven. The bread crumbs are best used immediately. Allow any leftovers to cool completely, and then store in a covered container in the pantry.

Per Serving (2 tablespoons): Calories: 27; Total Fat: 2g; Saturated Fat: 0g; Carbohydrates: 2g; Sodium: 58mg; Fiber: 0g; Protein: 0g

Cream of Broccoli Soup

EGG-FREE · GLUTEN-FREE · NUT-FREE

Serves 6

Prep time: 10 minutes / Cook time: 8 to 10 hours

Spicy red pepper flakes and bright lemon juice liven up the sweet, mellow flavor of slow-cooked broccoli in this healthy soup. I use chicken broth for more depth of flavor and body, but if you prefer to keep it vegetarian, the Essential Vegetable Broth (page 14) is equally delicious.

4 heads broccoli, trimmed and coarsely chopped

1 cup diced yellow onion

6 garlic cloves, smashed

¼ teaspoon red pepper flakes

Zest of 1 lemon

8 cups Chicken Broth (page 17) or store-bought

¾ cup full-fat plain Greek yogurt, plus more for serving

1. Put the broccoli, onion, garlic, red pepper flakes, lemon zest, and broth in the slow cooker. Stir, then cover and cook on low for 8 to 10 hours.

2. Turn off the slow cooker. Add the yogurt. Using an immersion blender, puree the soup until smooth.

3. Stir in additional Greek yogurt to serve. Divide the soup among serving bowls.

* **Time-Saving Prep Tip:** Chop the broccoli ahead of time, perhaps the night before. Not only will it save you time in the morning, but also it will improve the nutritional value of the soup thanks to the healthy compound sulforaphane, which develops after the broccoli is chopped.

Per Serving: Calories: 77; Total Fat: 2g; Saturated Fat: 0g; Carbohydrates: 14g; Sodium: 156mg; Fiber: 4g; Protein: 5g

Potato-Leek Soup

EGG-FREE • GLUTEN-FREE • NUT-FREE

Serves 6

Prep time: 5 minutes / Cook time: 8 to 10 hours

Who knew you could enjoy classic French cuisine without spending hours in the kitchen? This traditional pureed soup combines fragrant, subtle leeks with Yukon gold potatoes, fresh herbs, and luxurious heavy cream. If you have any leftovers, they're equally delicious served chilled or reheated.

2 large leeks, trimmed, washed, and coarsely chopped (see prep tip)

1 pound Yukon gold potatoes, peeled and diced

1 yellow onion, diced

2 garlic cloves, smashed

2 fresh thyme sprigs

1 bay leaf

8 cups Chicken Broth (page 17) or store-bought

½ cup heavy cream

Sea salt

Freshly ground black pepper

1. Put the leeks, potatoes, onion, garlic, thyme, bay leaf, and broth in the slow cooker. Stir, then cover and cook on low for 8 to 10 hours.

2. Turn off the slow cooker. Remove the thyme and bay leaf. Stir in the heavy cream. Using an immersion blender, puree the soup until smooth. Taste and adjust the seasoning, if needed. Divide among serving bowls.

Time-Saving Prep Tip: To prepare the leeks, cut off the root ends and then slice in half lengthwise. Rinse the leeks under cool running water, peeling away the layers so the water fully cleans between them. You don't have to peel them apart, just enough to let the water remove any trapped dirt.

Flavor Tip: For an extra bit of decadence, cook about 2 ounces diced bacon or pancetta over low heat for about 10 minutes, or until it renders most of its fat. Set on a paper towel to drain and then sprinkle a little over each bowl of soup.

Per Serving: Calories: 154; Total Fat: 7g; Saturated Fat: 5g; Carbohydrates: 20g; Sodium: 145mg; Fiber: 3g; Protein: 3g

Cannellini Bean and Cheddar Bisque

EGG-FREE • GLUTEN-FREE • NUT-FREE

Serves 6

Prep time: 5 minutes / Cook time: 8 to 10 hours

Cannellini beans provide a subtle, protein-packed backdrop for the sharp Cheddar cheese in this creamy soup. It's the love child of mac 'n' cheese and bean dip in soup form. Don't think about it too much. Just make it.

2 (15-ounce) cans cannellini beans, drained
1 yellow onion, diced
1 celery stalk, diced
1 garlic clove, smashed

1 tablespoon tomato paste
2 fresh thyme sprigs
8 cups Chicken Broth (page 17) or store-bought

2 cups whole milk
2 cups sharp Cheddar cheese
Sea salt
Freshly ground black pepper

1. Put the beans, onion, celery, garlic, tomato paste, thyme, and broth in the slow cooker. Stir, then cover and cook on low for 8 to 10 hours.

2. Turn off the slow cooker. Remove the thyme sprigs.

3. Add the milk. Using an immersion blender, puree the soup until smooth.

4. Stir in the cheese until it is thoroughly melted. Taste and adjust the seasoning, if needed. Divide the soup among serving bowls.

✳ **Flavor Tip:** Wondering why the milk isn't added at the beginning of the cooking time? It's because dairy products have a tendency to curdle in a slow cooker, even full-fat dairy, so stir it in near the end of the cooking time. It can withstand about 30 to 60 minutes of cooking.

Per Serving: Calories: 393; Total Fat: 16g; Saturated Fat: 9g; Carbohydrates: 39g; Sodium: 384mg; Fiber: 10g; Protein: 24g

Tortilla Soup

DAIRY-FREE ◦ EGG-FREE ◦ GLUTEN-FREE ◦ NUT-FREE

Serves 6

Prep time: 5 minutes / Cook time: 8 to 10 hours

Starchy corn tortillas thicken this easy Mexican soup. But let's be honest, it's really all about the toppings: crumbled Cotija, loads of corn tortilla strips, and aromatic cilantro offer a nice variety of flavor and texture.

1 yellow onion, diced

4 corn tortillas, ripped into pieces

4 garlic cloves, smashed

1 jalapeño pepper, coarsely chopped

1 tablespoon ground cumin

1 tablespoon smoked paprika

½ teaspoon sea salt, plus more as needed

1 (15-ounce) can fire-roasted diced tomatoes

8 cups Chicken Broth (page 17) or store-bought

Freshly ground black pepper

2 cups shredded cooked chicken

1 cup frozen fire-roasted corn, thawed

Coarsely chopped fresh cilantro, for serving

Sliced radishes, for serving

Tortilla strips, for serving

Peeled, pitted, and diced ripe avocado, for serving

½ cup Cotija cheese, crumbled, for serving (optional)

1 lime, cut into wedges, for serving

1. Put the onion, tortillas, garlic, jalapeño, cumin, paprika, salt, tomatoes, and broth in the slow cooker. Stir, then cover and cook on low for 8 to 10 hours.

2. Turn off the slow cooker. Using an immersion blender, puree the soup until smooth. Taste and adjust the seasoning, if needed.

3. Stir in the chicken and corn. Divide the soup among serving bowls.

4. Top each bowl with cilantro, radishes, tortilla strips, avocado, and cheese (if using). Serve with lime wedges.

Per Serving: Calories: 158; Total Fat: 3g; Saturated Fat: 1g; Carbohydrates: 18g; Sodium: 314mg; Fiber: 4g; Protein: 16g

Spinach and Apple Soup with Crumbled Bacon

EGG-FREE • GLUTEN-FREE • NUT-FREE

Serves 4 to 6

Prep time: 10 minutes / Cook time: 8 to 10 hours, plus 10 minutes to cook the bacon

This recipe requires just a little more prep work than the others, but it's worth it. Rendered fat from applewood-smoked bacon combines with the vegetable soup while it simmers all day. Then the bacon is crumbled on top with goat cheese. The Russet potato provides just the right amount of starch to thicken the soup.

2 applewood-smoked bacon slices

2 cups diced apples

1 Russet potato, peeled and diced

1 yellow onion, diced

1 garlic clove, smashed

¼ teaspoon sea salt, plus more as needed

4 cups Chicken Broth (page 17) or store-bought

8 cups spinach, coarsely chopped

¼ cup coarsely chopped fresh flat-leaf parsley

Freshly ground black pepper

2 ounces goat cheese, crumbled

1. Put the bacon in a medium skillet, and cook over medium-low heat for about 10 minutes, or until it has rendered most of its fat and cooked through. Remove from the heat. Set the bacon aside to cool, then crumble and refrigerate until ready to serve.

2. Pour 1 tablespoon of rendered bacon fat into the slow cooker, then add the apples, potato, onion, garlic, salt, and broth. Stir, then cover and cook on low for 8 to 10 hours.

3. Turn off the slow cooker. Stir in the spinach and parsley. Cover, and let braise in the hot liquid for about 1 minute, or until wilted. Using an immersion blender, puree the soup until smooth. Taste and adjust the seasoning, if needed. Divide among serving bowls.

4. Top each bowl with the crumbled bacon and goat cheese.

✳ **Variation Tip:** To make this soup vegan, omit the bacon, replace the chicken broth with vegetable broth, and use a plant-based cheese, such as Kite Hill or Miyoko's Creamery, in place of the goat cheese.

Per Serving: Calories: 219; Total Fat: 9g; Saturated Fat: 2g; Carbohydrates: 30g; Sodium: 427mg; Fiber: 4g; Protein: 9g

French Onion Soup with Gruyère Crostini
pages 56–57

CHAPTER 4

Vegetable and Bean Soups

Minestrone 45

Tuscan Bread Soup 46

Coconut Curried Vegetable Soup 47

Yellow Dal 48

   BONUS: Tadka 49

Spicy Lentil Soup 50

Chipotle and Black Bean Soup 51

Miso and Kabocha Squash Soup 52

Wild Rice and Mushroom Soup 53

Split Pea Soup 54

Cumin-Scented Chickpea and Tequila Soup 55

French Onion Soup 56

   BONUS: Gruyère Crostini 57

Vibrant Chickpea Coconut Curry 58

Simmered Pinto Beans with Avocado 59

Minestrone

DAIRY-FREE • EGG-FREE • NUT-FREE • VEGAN

Serves 6

Prep time: 10 minutes / Cook time: 8 to 10 hours

Minestrone soup in a slow cooker is a slightly daunting proposition. Add the pasta at the beginning, and it turns to mush before the cooking is done. Add it at the end, and it could take 20 minutes to be fully cooked, depending on how hot your slow cooker gets. I found a brilliant alternative in wheat berries. They cook slowly with the other ingredients and are even healthier than refined pasta.

1 yellow onion, diced

1 carrot, minced

1 celery stalk, minced

6 garlic cloves, minced

¼ cup minced fresh flat-leaf parsley

1 teaspoon minced fresh thyme

Pinch red pepper flakes

2 (15-ounce) cans kidney beans, drained and rinsed

1 (28-ounce) can whole plum tomatoes, coarsely chopped, juices reserved

1 gallon Essential Vegetable Broth (page 14) or store-bought

8 ounces wheat berries

Sea salt

Freshly ground black pepper

1. Put the onion, carrot, celery, garlic, parsley, thyme, red pepper flakes, beans, tomatoes with their juices, broth, and wheat berries in the slow cooker. Stir, then cover and cook on low for 8 to 10 hours.

2. Turn off the slow cooker. Taste and adjust the seasoning, if needed. Divide the soup among serving bowls.

✳ **Variation Tip:** To make this soup gluten-free, look for a gluten-free orzo pasta or another small shape, such as shells.

Per Serving: Calories: 186; Total Fat: 0g; Saturated Fat: 0g; Carbohydrates: 36g; Sodium: 152mg; Fiber: 10g; Protein: 11g

Tuscan Bread Soup

DAIRY-FREE · EGG-FREE · NUT-FREE · VEGAN

Serves 6
Prep time: 15 minutes / Cook time: 8 to 10 hours

Bread in soup? Yes! Not only is it a frugal way to use up stale bread, but also it's a tasty way to thicken your soup without making a roux. Although the soup is vegan, it tastes as if it is thickened with heavy cream.

2 (28-ounce) cans plum tomatoes

1 yellow onion, diced

6 garlic cloves, minced

½ cup minced fresh herbs, such as parsley, rosemary, thyme, and basil

4 French bread slices, crusts removed, cubed

1 (15-ounce) can cannellini beans or another white bean, drained and rinsed

4 cups coarsely chopped kale, ribs removed

8 cups Essential Vegetable Broth (page 14)

¼ cup extra-virgin olive oil, plus more for serving

½ teaspoon sea salt, plus more as needed

Freshly ground black pepper

1. Pour the tomatoes with their juices into the slow cooker. Using your clean hands, tear the tomatoes into pieces.

2. Add the onion, garlic, herbs, bread, beans, kale, broth, oil, and salt. Stir, then cover and cook on low for 8 to 10 hours.

3. Turn off the slow cooker. Taste and adjust the seasoning, if needed. Divide the soup among serving bowls.

4. Drizzle each bowl with additional olive oil, if desired.

* **Time-Saving Prep Tip:** There's a lot of chopping vegetables for this recipe. Get that done the night before to cut down on prep time and dishes in the morning.

Per Serving: Calories: 296; Total Fat: 11g; Saturated Fat: 2g; Carbohydrates: 42g; Sodium: 554mg; Fiber: 11g; Protein: 12g

Coconut Curried Vegetable Soup

DAIRY-FREE · EGG-FREE · GLUTEN-FREE · VEGAN

Serves 6

Prep time: 15 minutes / Cook time: 8 to 10 hours

A long, slow cook time transforms vegetables until they're soft, succulent, and almost unrecognizable as they melt into the broth. To make this soup into a more substantial meal, stir in 1 pound peeled shrimp after the soup has cooked for 8 hours, and cook for 3 to 5 minutes, or just until opaque.

4 zucchini, diced

4 medium sweet
  potatoes, peeled
  and diced

4 carrots, diced

1 yellow onion, minced

3 garlic cloves, minced

1 cup brown jasmine rice

1 tablespoon minced
  fresh ginger

1 tablespoon
  curry powder

½ teaspoon sea salt, plus
  more as needed

2 (15-ounce) cans
  full-fat coconut milk

8 cups Essential
  Vegetable
  Broth (page 14)
  or store-bought

Freshly ground
  black pepper

1. Put the zucchini, sweet potatoes, carrots, onion, garlic, rice, ginger, curry powder, salt, coconut milk, and broth in the slow cooker. Stir, then cover and cook on low for 8 to 10 hours.

2. Turn off the slow cooker. Taste and adjust the seasoning, if needed. Divide the soup among serving bowls.

Substitution Tip: This soup includes brown jasmine rice, but go ahead and use a long-grain brown rice if that's what you have.

Per Serving: Calories: 567; Total Fat: 35g; Saturated Fat: 30g; Carbohydrates: 60g; Sodium: 405mg; Fiber: 10g; Protein: 10g

Yellow Dal

DAIRY-FREE • EGG-FREE • GLUTEN-FREE • NUT-FREE • VEGETARIAN

Serves 6

Prep time: 5 minutes / Cook time: 8 to 10 hours

Traditionally, dal isn't a soup at all. It functions more like a sauce that you might sop up with naan or ladle over rice. Nevertheless, it has such a delicious texture and flavor, it works equally well thinned out just a bit and served with bread, rice, and tadka, a loose blend of toasted spices and oil (recipe follows).

2 cups split yellow lentils

1 cup minced
  yellow onion

1 garlic clove, minced

2 teaspoons
  ground turmeric

1 teaspoon
  ground coriander

½ teaspoon sea salt

8 cups Essential
  Vegetable
  Broth (page 14)
  or store-bought

½ cup minced cilantro,
  for serving

½ cup Tadka (recipe
  follows), for serving

1. Put the lentils, onion, garlic, turmeric, coriander, salt, and broth in the slow cooker. Stir, then cover and cook on low for 8 to 10 hours.

2. Turn off the slow cooker. Divide the dal among serving bowls.

3. Top each bowl with the cilantro and tadka.

Per Serving: Calories: 320; Total Fat: 8g; Saturated Fat: 1g; Carbohydrates: 47g; Sodium: 204mg; Fiber: 9g; Protein: 17g

Tadka

Makes ½ cup

Prep time: 5 minutes / Cook time: 10 minutes

2 tablespoons ghee or canola oil

1 tablespoon whole cumin seed

1 cinnamon stick

½ teaspoon red pepper flakes

1 red onion, diced

1. In a large skillet, heat the ghee over medium-high heat.
2. When the ghee is hot, add the cumin, cinnamon, and red pepper flakes. Cook for 30 seconds to 1 minute, or just until fragrant. Be careful not to burn.
3. Reduce the heat to medium-low. Add the onion, and cook for 7 to 10 minutes, or until nearly soft. Remove from the heat.

Per Serving (2 tablespoons): Calories: 79; Total Fat: 7g; Saturated Fat: 1g; Carbohydrates: 3g; Sodium: 4mg; Fiber: 1g; Protein: 1g

Spicy Lentil Soup

DAIRY-FREE ● EGG-FREE ● GLUTEN-FREE ● NUT-FREE ● VEGAN

Serves 6

Prep time: 5 minutes / Cook time: 8 to 10 hours

This simple vegan soup has become a staple in my kitchen. And the slow cooker makes it even easier because I don't even have to light up a burner on the stove. Use Puy lentils, also known as French green lentils, which won't completely disintegrate into the soup. See the tip for serving suggestions.

2 cups Puy lentils
2 yellow onions, minced
2 garlic cloves, minced
2 tablespoons
  curry powder
2 tablespoons canola oil

½ teaspoon sea salt
8 cups Essential
  Vegetable
  Broth (page 14)
  or store-bought

Coarsely chopped fresh
  parsley, for serving

1. Put the lentils, onions, garlic, curry powder, oil, salt, and broth in the slow cooker. Stir, then cover and cook on low for 8 to 10 hours.
2. Turn off the slow cooker. Divide the soup among serving bowls.
3. Top each bowl with parsley.

   Flavor Tip: If you have the time to prepare a few garnishes, they really take this soup from plain Jane to over the top! Try a poached egg, a drizzle of yogurt, minced red onions, and cilantro.

Per Serving: Calories: 290; Total Fat: 6g; Saturated Fat: 1g; Carbohydrates: 45g; Sodium: 300mg; Fiber: 9g; Protein: 6g

Chipotle and Black Bean Soup

DAIRY-FREE • EGG-FREE • GLUTEN-FREE • NUT-FREE • VEGAN

Serves 6

Prep time: 10 minutes / Cook time: 8 to 10 hours

Chipotle peppers are dried, smoked jalapeño peppers. You can find them dried, but they're challenging to use in cooking without a proper spice grinder. Chipotles in adobo have the same heat and smokiness, but they also have an addictive tang thanks to the vinegar in the adobo sauce. They permeate this soup with their smoky, spicy goodness, making even the humble black bean sing with flavor. Serve with diced avocados, sour cream, or crema to cool things off.

4 (15-ounce) cans black beans, drained

1 yellow onion, diced

1 celery stalk, minced

1 red bell pepper, diced

4 garlic cloves, minced

1 chipotle in adobo sauce, plus 1 to 3 teaspoons adobo sauce

1 tablespoon smoked paprika

1 teaspoon ground cumin

½ teaspoon sea salt, plus more as needed

8 cups Essential Vegetable Broth (page 14) or store-bought

Freshly ground black pepper

1. Put the beans, onion, celery, bell pepper, garlic, chipotle in adobo with sauce, paprika, cumin, salt, and broth in the slow cooker. Stir, then cover and cook on low for 8 to 10 hours.

2. Turn off the slow cooker. Remove 2 cups of soup to a blender, vent the lid, cover with a kitchen towel, and blend until smooth. Pour the mixture back into the slow cooker. Taste and adjust the seasoning, if needed. Divide among serving bowls.

Substitution Tip: If you follow a gluten-free diet, make sure to read the label carefully for the chipotles. Sometimes the adobo sauce is thickened with flour. If you can't find a gluten-free version, use 1 whole dried chipotle and 1 teaspoon vinegar. Remove the chipotle before serving.

Per Serving: Calories: 248; Total Fat: 1g; Saturated Fat: 0g; Carbohydrates: 45g; Sodium: 301mg; Fiber: 16g; Protein: 16g

Miso and Kabocha Squash Soup

DAIRY-FREE • EGG-FREE • GLUTEN-FREE • NUT-FREE

Serves 6

Prep time: 10 minutes / Cook time: 8 to 10 hours

Earthy kabocha squash and tender green cabbage meld beautifully in this Japanese hot pot. It is seasoned with sweet white miso and a splash of vinegar for brightness. If you can get your hands on a bottle of togarashi, or Japanese seven-spice powder, it adds a fragrant spicy flavor to the soup. It's made with seaweed, black sesame seeds, chiles, orange peel, Japanese pepper, and other seasonings. Serve at the table so each person can season to their liking.

1 kabocha squash, halved, seeded, and cut into 2-inch chunks

½ savoy or green cabbage, cut into 2-inch chunks

1 yellow onion, halved and thinly sliced from stem to roots

2 garlic cloves, smashed

1 teaspoon minced fresh ginger

8 cups Chicken Broth (page 17) or store-bought

4 boneless skinless chicken thighs

¼ cup white miso

2 tablespoons tahini

1 tablespoon rice vinegar

½ cup coarsely chopped fresh basil, for serving

2 scallions, white and green parts, thinly sliced, for serving

1. Put the squash, cabbage, onion, garlic, ginger, broth, and chicken in the slow cooker. Stir, then cover and cook on low for 8 to 10 hours.

2. Turn off the slow cooker. Remove a ladleful of the broth to a small bowl.

3. Whisk the miso, tahini, and vinegar into the bowl. Pour into the slow cooker, and mix well. Divide the soup among serving dishes.

4. Top each dish with basil and scallions.

 * **Variation Tip:** To make this soup vegetarian, replace the chicken thighs and chicken broth with vegetable broth and 1 (15-ounce) can chickpeas.

Per Serving: Calories: 196; Total Fat: 6g; Saturated Fat: 1g; Carbohydrates: 17g; Sodium: 484mg; Fiber: 4g; Protein: 21g

Wild Rice and Mushroom Soup

Serves 6

Prep time: 5 minutes / Cook time: 8 to 10 hours

I love the earthiness of this filling rice and mushroom soup. Wild rice stands up well to the long cooking time compared to brown or white rice. And it's the perfect complement to earthy cremini mushrooms. They're the immature version of portabella mushrooms, and either will work. You can also use button mushrooms, if you like.

2 cups wild rice

8 ounces cremini mushrooms, finely diced

1 yellow onion, minced

4 garlic cloves, minced

2 tablespoons butter

1 teaspoon minced fresh rosemary

1 teaspoon minced fresh thyme

½ teaspoon sea salt, plus more as needed

8 cups Mushroom Stock (page 15) or store-bought

4 cups Chicken Broth (page 17) or store-bought

Freshly ground black pepper

½ cup coarsely chopped fresh flat-leaf parsley, for serving

2 lemons, cut into wedges, for serving

1. Put the rice, mushrooms, onion, garlic, butter, rosemary, thyme, salt, mushroom stock, and chicken broth in the slow cooker. Stir, then cover and cook on low for 8 to 10 hours.

2. Turn off the slow cooker. Taste and adjust the seasoning, if needed. Divide the soup among serving bowls.

3. Top each bowl with parsley, and serve with the lemon wedges.

* **Substitution Tip:** If you don't have mushroom stock on hand, use an additional 8 cups chicken broth instead.

Per Serving: Calories: 251; Total Fat: 5g; Saturated Fat: 3g; Carbohydrates: 45g; Sodium: 341mg; Fiber: 5g; Protein: 10g

Split Pea Soup

DAIRY-FREE ● EGG-FREE ● GLUTEN-FREE ● NUT-FREE

Serves 6

Prep time: 5 minutes / Cook time: 8 to 10 hours

Split pea soup was made for the slow cooker. A salty, smoky ham hock infuses the broth with flavor while the peas slowly tenderize and melt into a sweet, chunky soup. Serve with crusty bread and a cold beer for a hearty winter meal.

1 ham hock
2 cups split peas
1 teaspoon minced
  fresh thyme

1 cup minced red onion
1 garlic clove, smashed
1 bay leaf

8 cups Chicken
  Broth (page 17)
  or store-bought

1. Put the ham hock, peas, thyme, onion, garlic, bay leaf, and broth in the slow cooker. Stir, then cover and cook on low for 8 to 10 hours.

2. Turn off the slow cooker. Remove the ham hock and bay leaf. Divide the soup among serving bowls.

* **Substitution Tip:** For a plant-based soup, use vegetable broth. Swap out the ham hock for ½ teaspoon liquid smoke, and add 2 tablespoons canola oil to replace the fat from the meat.

Per Serving: Calories: 272; Total Fat: 2g; Saturated Fat: 0g; Carbohydrates: 45g; Sodium: 385mg; Fiber: 17g; Protein: 21g

Cumin-Scented Chickpea and Tequila Soup

DAIRY-FREE ∘ EGG-FREE ∘ GLUTEN-FREE ∘ NUT-FREE

Serves 6

Prep time: 5 minutes / Cook time: 8 to 10 hours

I cook frequently with white and red wine, but I rarely have liquor in the house and so never think to cook with it. This soup changed my mind. It's worth going out and buying a bottle. The first time I made it, our neighbors had just given us a bottle of mezcal. The smokiness of the agave-based liquor was perfect for this soup. Either tequila or mezcal will work.

4 ripe tomatoes, diced
1 red onion, halved and thinly sliced from stem to roots
6 garlic cloves, minced
1 minced chipotle in adobo sauce
¼ cup tequila or mezcal

1 tablespoon ground cumin
2 teaspoons smoked paprika
2 (15-ounce) cans chickpeas, drained

8 cups Chicken Broth (page 17) or store-bought
Coarsely chopped fresh cilantro, for serving
2 ripe avocados, peeled, pitted, and diced, for serving

1. Put the tomatoes, onion, garlic, chipotle in adobo, tequila, cumin, paprika, chickpeas, and broth in the slow cooker. Stir, then cover and cook on low for 8 to 10 hours.
2. Turn off the slow cooker. Divide among serving bowls.
3. Top each bowl with cilantro, and serve with the avocado.

Flavor Tip: Many recipes call for rinsing chickpeas. However, the liquid that clings to them is called aquafaba and has thickening properties that enhance the texture of the soup.

Per Serving: Calories: 300; Total Fat: 13g; Saturated Fat: 2g; Carbohydrates: 35g; Sodium: 319mg; Fiber: 13g; Protein: 10g

French Onion Soup

EGG-FREE • GLUTEN-FREE • NUT-FREE

Serves 6
Prep time: 10 minutes / Cook time: 8 to 10 hours,
plus 5 minutes to heat the broth

I learned to make French onion soup from Julia Child's cookbook *Mastering the Art of French Cooking*. Of course, it was perfection. But because it took so long to cook and required standing at the stove the entire time, I only made it a couple times. Who has the time for that with a newborn? I sure didn't. The slow cooker works like magic to caramelize the onions all day. Then stir in the beef broth, serve with crostini, and call it a meal.

6 large yellow onions,
  halved and thinly sliced
  from stem to roots
2 tablespoons butter

2 tablespoons canola oil
1 teaspoon sugar
1 teaspoon minced
  fresh thyme

¼ cup dry white wine
8 cups Beef
  Stock (page 18)
  or store-bought

1. Put the onions, butter, oil, sugar, and thyme in the slow cooker. Stir, then cover and cook on low for 8 to 10 hours.

2. Add the wine, and cook, stirring, for 2 minutes, or until some of the alcohol has evaporated.

3. Stir in the beef stock, bring to a simmer, and cook for about 2 minutes. The flavor will continue to deepen as it cooks, but it can be served immediately if you prefer.

4. Turn off the slow cooker. Divide the soup among serving bowls. Serve with Gruyère Crostini (recipe follows).

* **Substitution Tip:** If you prefer to avoid alcohol, use 1 tablespoon white-wine vinegar or apple cider instead of the wine.

Per Serving: Calories: 146; Total Fat: 9g; Saturated Fat: 3g; Carbohydrates: 15g; Sodium: 136mg; Fiber: 3g; Protein: 2g

Gruyère Crostini

EGG-FREE • NUT-FREE

Makes 6 slices
Prep time: 5 minutes / Cook time: 1 to 2 minutes

6 French bread slices   6 Gruyère
                             cheese slices

1. Preheat the broiler on high.
2. Spread the bread slices out on a broiler pan. Top each piece of bread with a slice of Gruyère. Broil for 1 to 2 minutes, or until the cheese has slightly browned. Remove from the broiler.

Per Serving: Calories: 193; Total Fat: 9g; Saturated Fat: 5g; Carbohydrates: 18g; Sodium: 212mg; Fiber: 1g; Protein: 11g

Vibrant Chickpea Coconut Curry

DAIRY-FREE ● EGG-FREE ● GLUTEN-FREE

Serves 6

Prep time: 5 minutes / Cook time: 8 to 10 hours

I made this stew when I had just moved into my new house in Oceanside, California. Even after 12 years of cooking for a husband and kids, it was a rare occurrence when the whole family was happy with dinner. Most evenings involved me generating an entire sink of dishes to prepare something that satisfied everyone's taste, or I ended up listening to complaining throughout the meal. What a delight to find an easy, healthy soup the whole family loves!

2 yellow onions, minced

6 garlic cloves, smashed

2 teaspoons ground turmeric

1 teaspoon ground coriander

½ teaspoon sea salt

¼ teaspoon red pepper flakes

2 (15-ounce) cans chickpeas, drained

2 (15-ounce) cans full-fat coconut milk

4 cups Chicken Broth (page 17) or store-bought

4 cups baby spinach

1. Put the onions, garlic, turmeric, coriander, salt, red pepper flakes, chickpeas, coconut milk, and broth in the slow cooker. Stir, then cover and cook on low for 8 to 10 hours.

2. Turn off the slow cooker. Stir in the spinach, and let wilt, about 1 minute. Divide the soup among serving bowls.

   ❋ **Flavor Tip:** The coconut milk has a tendency to separate a bit while cooking. Stir the soup with a wooden spoon before serving to emulsify it.

Per Serving: Calories: 441; Total Fat: 33g; Saturated Fat: 27g; Carbohydrates: 32g; Sodium: 336mg; Fiber: 8g; Protein: 11g

Simmered Pinto Beans with Avocado

DAIRY-FREE ● EGG-FREE ● GLUTEN-FREE ● NUT-FREE

Serves 6

Prep time: 5 minutes / Cook time: 8 to 10 hours

A simple soup of beans topped with avocado and tomato is just what I'm looking for when life feels like it's going too fast. When work pressures stack up. When the kids have problems at school. When nothing seems to be going right, I know that with just a handful of pantry staples, I'm moments (okay, in this case unattended hours) away from a healthy dinner. It's such a comfort.

2 (28-ounce) cans pinto beans, drained
1 yellow onion, minced
4 garlic cloves, minced
1 tablespoon dried Mexican oregano

8 cups Chicken Broth (page 17) or store-bought
Sea salt
Freshly ground black pepper

2 ripe avocados, peeled, pitted, and diced, for serving
2 large tomatoes, diced, for serving
Juice of 2 limes, for serving

1. Put the beans, onion, garlic, oregano, and broth in the slow cooker. Stir, then cover and cook on low for 8 to 10 hours.

2. Turn off the slow cooker. Taste and adjust the seasoning, if needed. Divide the beans among serving bowls.

3. Top with the avocados, tomatoes, and lime juice.

Per Serving: Calories: 391; Total Fat: 11g; Saturated Fat: 2g; Carbohydrates: 59g; Sodium: 108mg; Fiber: 22g; Protein: 19g

Chicken Pho
page 74

CHAPTER 5

Pasta and Grain Soups

Fennel and Farro Soup 62

Quinoa and Sweet Potato Soup 63

Tres Chiles Grain Soup 64

Creamy Wild Rice Soup 65

Truffle-Mushroom Risotto Soup 66

    BONUS: Kale Salad 67

Pasta e Fagioli 68

Farro and Chicken Soup 69

Sticky Rice and Ginger-Chicken Porridge 70

Chorizo and Wild Rice Soup 71

Arroz Caldo 72

Chicken Pho 74

Tender Pork Posole 76

Italian Wedding Soup 79

Persian Lamb and Rice Soup 80

Beef and Barley Soup 81

Fennel and Farro Soup

DAIRY-FREE ● EGG-FREE ● NUT-FREE ● VEGAN

Serves 6

Prep time: 10 minutes / Cook time: 8 hours

This soup has a subtle elegance. Tender fennel bulb infuses the broth and chewy farro with anise flavor. Serve with pan-seared halibut or another firm white fish for a complete meal. Or top with crumbled plant-based cheese for a vegan meal.

1½ cups pearled farro
1 fennel bulb, cored, halved, and thinly sliced, fronds reserved for garnish
¼ cup dry white wine

2 shallots, minced
1 garlic clove, minced
½ teaspoon fennel seeds, lightly crushed

8 cups Essential Vegetable Broth (page 14) or store-bought
Sea salt
Freshly ground black pepper

1. Put the farro, fennel bulb, wine, shallots, garlic, fennel seeds, and broth in the slow cooker. Stir, then cover and cook on low for 8 hours.

2. Turn off the slow cooker. Taste and adjust the seasoning, if needed. Divide the soup among serving bowls.

3. Top each bowl with the reserved fennel fronds.

  ✳ **Variation Tip:** To braise fish without dirtying another dish, season 4 to 6 halibut fillets with salt and pepper, put in the soup, cover, and braise for 5 to 7 minutes, or until cooked through.

Per Serving: Calories: 143; Total Fat: 1g; Saturated Fat: 0g; Carbohydrates: 31g; Sodium: 127mg; Fiber: 6g; Protein: 5g

Quinoa and Sweet Potato Soup

DAIRY-FREE · EGG-FREE · GLUTEN-FREE · NUT-FREE · VEGAN

Serves 6

Prep time: 10 minutes / Cook time: 8 hours

This healthy soup has it all—protein-rich quinoa, smoked paprika, sweet potatoes, fresh spinach, and a pop of yellow corn. It's plant-based and gluten-free, making it a healthy weeknight dinner. The long, slow cooking time softens the sweet potatoes until they virtually dissolve into the soup. If you prefer firmer vegetables, you can stop the cooking as early as 5 to 6 hours.

2 cups diced peeled sweet potatoes (about 3 small sweet potatoes)
1 cup quinoa
1 yellow onion, minced
4 garlic cloves, minced
1 tablespoon smoked paprika
1 teaspoon ground cumin

½ teaspoon sea salt, plus more as needed
8 cups Essential Vegetable Broth (page 14) or store-bought
1 cup fresh or frozen corn kernels, thawed if frozen

2 cups shredded spinach
½ cup coarsely chopped fresh cilantro
Freshly ground black pepper
2 limes, cut into wedges, for serving

1. Put the sweet potatoes, quinoa, onion, garlic, paprika, cumin, salt, and broth in the slow cooker. Stir, then cover and cook on low for 8 hours.

2. Turn off the slow cooker. Stir in the corn, spinach, and cilantro. Taste and adjust the seasoning, if needed. Divide the soup among serving bowls.

3. Serve the soup with the lime wedges.

Per Serving: Calories: 183; Total Fat: 2g; Saturated Fat: 0g; Carbohydrates: 36g; Sodium: 381mg; Fiber: 5g; Protein: 6g

Tres Chiles Grain Soup

EGG-FREE • GLUTEN-FREE • NUT-FREE • VEGETARIAN

Serves 6

Prep time: 10 minutes / Cook time: 6 to 8 hours

This fiery Mexican grain-based soup showcases the diversity of flavors and levels of heat in three different chiles: poblano, chipotle, and jalapeño. Cool things off by topping the soup with a drizzle of sour cream and diced avocado.

1 (15-ounce) can fire-roasted diced tomatoes
1 cup short-grain brown rice
½ cup pearl barley
1 yellow onion, diced
1 small zucchini, diced
1 carrot, diced
1 cup diced mushrooms
4 garlic cloves, minced

2 poblano peppers, cored, seeded, and diced
1 chipotle in adobo sauce, minced, plus 1 teaspoon adobo sauce
1 jalapeño pepper, minced

12 cups Essential Vegetable Broth (page 14) or store-bought
Sea salt
Freshly ground black pepper
Coarsely chopped fresh cilantro, for serving
Sour cream, for serving
Peeled, pitted, and diced ripe avocado, for serving

1. Put the tomatoes, rice, barley, onion, zucchini, carrot, mushrooms, garlic, poblano peppers, chipotle and adobo sauce, jalapeño, and broth in the slow cooker. Stir, then cover and cook on low for 6 to 8 hours.

2. Turn off the slow cooker. Taste and adjust the seasoning, if needed. Divide the soup among serving bowls.

3. Serve the soup with cilantro, sour cream, and avocado.

❋ **Substitution Tip:** If you can't find one of the chiles, consult the Scoville scale, which measures the heat of peppers. Choose one that has a similar heat profile as a substitute.

Per Serving: Calories: 313; Total Fat: 10g; Saturated Fat: 3g; Carbohydrates: 51g; Sodium: 205mg; Fiber: 9g; Protein: 7g

Creamy Wild Rice Soup

EGG-FREE ● GLUTEN-FREE ● VEGETARIAN

Serves 6

Prep time: 10 minutes / Cook time: 8 to 10 hours

Wild rice is even more nutritious than brown rice, with fewer calories and more protein. Coupled with butternut squash, it makes for a healthy meatless main dish. In a slow cooker on low heat, butternut squash disintegrates into the richly spiced broth, thickening it and bringing an earthy flavor and beautiful color.

4 cups diced
   butternut squash
1 cup diced
   fresh tomatoes
1½ cups wild rice
1 yellow onion, minced
2 garlic cloves, minced
2 teaspoons
   curry powder

¼ teaspoon red
   pepper flakes
1 (15-ounce) can full-fat
   coconut milk
12 cups Essential
   Vegetable Broth
   (page 14) or store-
   bought
Sea salt

Freshly ground
   black pepper
Handful fresh mint,
   thinly sliced, for serving
1 cup full-fat plain
   yogurt, for serving

1. Put the squash, tomatoes, rice, onion, garlic, curry powder, red pepper flakes, coconut milk, and broth in the slow cooker. Stir, then cover and cook on low for 8 to 10 hours.

2. Turn off the heat. Taste and adjust the seasoning, if needed. Divide the soup among serving bowls.

3. Top each bowl with fresh mint and a drizzle of yogurt.

   Variation Tip: If you're serving children, omit the red pepper flakes, and serve with chili-garlic sauce on the side at the table.

Per Serving: Calories: 366; Total Fat: 17g; Saturated Fat: 14g; Carbohydrates: 48g; Sodium: 147mg; Fiber: 5g; Protein: 10g

Truffle-Mushroom Risotto Soup

EGG-FREE · GLUTEN-FREE · NUT-FREE

Serves 6

Prep time: 10 minutes / Cook time: 8 to 10 hours

When making traditional risotto, you stir short-grain white rice continuously for 30 to 45 minutes while constantly adding hot broth. The starches in the rice are released, resulting in a rich, creamy dish. This version transforms risotto into a slow-cooked porridge-like soup, thickened by the rice starch. Fragrant thyme, mushrooms, and truffle salt make it a comfort food classic. Serve it with Kale Salad (recipe follows) to balance the rich flavors with a bright burst of acid.

2 cups coarsely chopped cremini mushrooms

1½ cups Arborio or short-grain white rice

1 yellow onion, minced

4 garlic cloves, minced

2 tablespoons butter

2 teaspoons minced fresh thyme

2 teaspoons minced fresh rosemary

1 teaspoon truffle salt

12 cups Essential Vegetable Broth (page 14) or store-bought

Sea salt

Freshly ground black pepper

2 ounces parmesan cheese, for serving (optional)

1. Put the mushrooms, rice, onion, garlic, butter, thyme, rosemary, salt, and broth in the slow cooker. Stir, then cover and cook on low for 8 to 10 hours.

2. Turn off the slow cooker. Taste and adjust the seasoning, if needed. Divide the soup among serving bowls.

3. Serve the soup with the cheese (if using).

* **Flavor Tip:** Use a vegetable peeler to shave off thin slices of parmesan to top the soup.

Per Serving: Calories: 231; Total Fat: 5g; Saturated Fat: 3g; Carbohydrates: 43g; Sodium: 421mg; Fiber: 2g; Protein: 5g

Kale Salad

DAIRY-FREE • EGG-FREE • GLUTEN-FREE • NUT-FREE • VEGAN

Serves 6
Prep time: 10 minutes

2 bunches Tuscan kale, tough stems removed, shredded

¼ teaspoon red pepper flakes

1 garlic clove, grated

1 teaspoon extra-virgin olive oil

Generous pinch sea salt

1 tablespoon freshly squeezed lemon juice

In a small bowl, combine the kale, red pepper flakes, garlic, oil, salt, and lemon juice. Using your clean hands, massage the kale until it softens and becomes deep green. Season with additional flaky sea salt, if desired.

Variation Tip: If you're serving children, omit the red pepper flakes and serve with chili-garlic sauce on the side at the table.

Per Serving: Calories: 13; Total Fat: 1g; Saturated Fat: 0g; Carbohydrates: 1g; Sodium: 24mg; Fiber: 0g; Protein: 1g

Pasta e Fagioli

DAIRY-FREE ● EGG-FREE ● NUT-FREE

Serves 6

Prep time: 10 minutes / Cook time: 8 hours, plus 10 minutes to cook the pasta

Tender beans and pork simmer in a rich vegetable broth in this version of the Italian classic, pasta e fagioli. Traditionally, the soup coincided with the annual pig slaughter. The recipe is all about making the most of all parts of the animal. This version calls for pancetta, but use what you can find. A pork shoulder also works well.

8 ounces pancetta, diced

½ cup dry white wine

4 cups cooked cranberry beans or pinto beans

1 yellow onion, minced

2 carrots, minced

1 celery stalk, minced

4 garlic cloves, minced

¼ cup minced fresh flat-leaf parsley

1 tablespoon minced fresh rosemary

2 bay leaves

1 gallon Chicken Broth (page 17) or store-bought

Sea salt

Freshly ground black pepper

8 ounces anelli pasta or macaroni

1. Heat a large skillet over medium heat.

2. Put the pancetta in the skillet, and cook until it renders most of its fat.

3. Add the wine, and cook for about 2 minutes. Remove from the heat. Scrape all of the mixture into the slow cooker.

4. Add the beans, onion, carrots, celery, garlic, parsley, rosemary, bay leaves, and broth. Stir, then cover and cook on low for 8 hours. Taste and adjust the seasoning, if needed.

5. Add the pasta, cover, and cook for 10 minutes.

6. Turn off the slow cooker. Remove and discard the bay leaves. Divide the soup among serving bowls.

Per Serving: Calories: 497; Total Fat: 16g; Saturated Fat: 5g; Carbohydrates: 64g; Sodium: 372mg; Fiber: 13g; Protein: 20g

Farro and Chicken Soup

Serves 6

Prep time: 10 minutes / Cook time: 8 to 10 hours

Farro is an ancient grain related to wheat. It has a nutty flavor and chewy texture, making it perfect for long, slow cooking times. In this soup, it's paired with bone-in chicken thighs (for maximum juiciness), fresh herbs, carrots, and celery. If that sounds a lot like chicken noodle soup to you, you're right. This version works much better in a slow cooker than one with egg noodles.

4 bone-in chicken thighs, skinned
1 cup pearled farro
2 carrots, diced
2 celery stalks, diced
6 garlic cloves, minced

1 teaspoon minced fresh thyme
½ teaspoon sea salt, plus more as needed
¼ teaspoon freshly ground black pepper, plus more as needed

12 cups Chicken Broth (page 17) or store-bought
Coarsely chopped fresh flat-leaf parsley, for serving

1. Put the chicken, farro, carrots, celery, garlic, thyme, salt, pepper, and broth in the slow cooker. Stir, then cover and cook on low for 8 to 10 hours.

2. Turn off the slow cooker. Remove the chicken, and place on a cutting board. When cool enough to handle, use two forks to shred the meat. Save the bones for another use. Return the meat to the slow cooker.

3. Stir in the parsley. Taste and adjust the seasoning, if needed. Divide the soup among serving bowls.

* **Substitution Tip:** If you prefer to use boneless chicken thighs, that's fine. Cut them into 2-inch pieces before adding them to the stew.

Per Serving: Calories: 249; Total Fat: 6g; Saturated Fat: 1g; Carbohydrates: 21g; Sodium: 439mg; Fiber: 4g; Protein: 28g

Sticky Rice and Ginger-Chicken Porridge

DAIRY-FREE • EGG-FREE • GLUTEN-FREE • NUT-FREE

Serves 6
Prep time: 5 minutes / Cook time: 6 to 8 hours

Fragrant ginger, pungent fish sauce, and aromatic spices bring life to sticky rice in this comforting porridge. Star anise is available in most well-stocked spice aisles. It's also sometimes available in bulk. If you can't find it, you can omit it or use about a teaspoon of fennel seeds, lightly crushed.

4 boneless skinless chicken thighs

1½ cups glutinous rice (aka sticky rice)

1 tablespoon minced fresh ginger

1 cinnamon stick

2 whole star anise

1½ tablespoons fish sauce

1 tablespoon brown sugar

4 cups Kombu Dashi (page 16)

8 cups Chicken Broth (page 17) or store-bought

Sea salt

Freshly ground black pepper

¼ cup minced fresh cilantro, for serving

1. Put the chicken, rice, ginger, cinnamon, star anise, fish sauce, sugar, kombu dashi, and broth in the slow cooker. Stir, then cover and cook on low for 6 to 8 hours.

2. Turn off the slow cooker. Remove the cinnamon stick and star anise. Taste and adjust the seasoning, if needed. Remove the chicken, and place on a cutting board. When cool enough to handle, use two forks to shred the meat. Return the meat to the slow cooker. Divide the porridge among serving bowls.

3. Top each bowl with cilantro.

* **Substitution Tip:** If you don't have time to make the kombu dashi, use 4 additional cups of chicken broth.

Per Serving: Calories: 338; Total Fat: 6g; Saturated Fat: 1g; Carbohydrates: 40g; Sodium: 480mg; Fiber: 1g; Protein: 28g

Chorizo and Wild Rice Soup

DAIRY-FREE · EGG-FREE · GLUTEN-FREE · NUT-FREE

Serves 6

Prep time: 10 minutes / Cook time: 8 to 10 hours

This simple wild rice soup is permeated with smoke and spice. Spanish chorizo infuses the soup with warm flavors and aromas, then a pinch of red pepper flakes amps up the heat, and smoked paprika rounds out the smoke. Fresh herbs and the sweet crunch of pomegranate provide the perfect finish.

1½ cups wild rice

4 ounces dried cured Spanish chorizo, casings removed, diced

1 yellow onion, minced

2 garlic cloves, minced

1 tablespoon minced fresh rosemary

1 teaspoon smoked paprika

¼ teaspoon red pepper flakes

12 cups Chicken Broth (page 17) or store-bought

Sea salt

Freshly ground black pepper

¼ cup minced fresh flat-leaf parsley, for serving

¼ cup minced fresh mint, for serving

1 cup pomegranate arils, for serving

1. Put the rice, chorizo, onion, garlic, rosemary, paprika, red pepper flakes, and broth in the slow cooker. Stir, then cover and cook on low for 8 to 10 hours.

2. Turn off the slow cooker. Taste and adjust the seasoning, if needed. Divide the soup among serving bowls.

3. Top each bowl with parsley, mint, and pomegranate.

Substitution Tip: If you prefer to use fresh chorizo instead of cured, cook it in a pan over medium-low heat, breaking up with a wooden spoon, for 5 to 7 minutes, or until cooked through and gently browned, before adding it to the slow cooker.

Per Serving: Calories: 264; Total Fat: 8g; Saturated Fat: 3g; Carbohydrates: 38g; Sodium: 240mg; Fiber: 4g; Protein: 11g

Arroz Caldo

DAIRY-FREE • GLUTEN-FREE • NUT-FREE

Serves 6

Prep time: 10 minutes / Cook time: 8 hours

Making this traditional Filipino soup in a slow cooker requires a bit of finessing to replicate the taste and texture of the original (see tip). Make sure to use a whole chicken when making the Chicken Broth (page 17) and reserve the chicken meat. Whatever you do, don't skip the garlic chips. Their caramelized taste and crunchy texture make even a slow-cooked arroz caldo feel authentic.

8 garlic cloves, divided

4 tablespoons canola oil, divided

2 cups glutinous rice (aka sticky rice)

2 tablespoons fish sauce

1 tablespoon minced fresh ginger

½ teaspoon sea salt, plus more as needed

Pinch saffron (optional)

8 cups Chicken Broth (page 17) or store-bought

Freshly ground black pepper

3 cups shredded cooked chicken, for serving

2 scallions, white and green parts, thinly sliced, for serving

3 hard-boiled eggs, peeled and halved, for serving

1. Mince 2 garlic cloves. Put the minced garlic, 2 tablespoons of oil, the sticky rice, fish sauce, ginger, salt, saffron (if using), and broth in the slow cooker. Stir, then cover and cook on low for 8 hours.

2. While the soup is cooking, make the garlic chips: Pour the remaining 2 tablespoons of oil into a medium shallow skillet. Thinly slice the remaining 6 garlic cloves, and add to the oil. Heat the oil over medium-low heat for about 5 minutes, or until the garlic begins to simmer and gently brown. Remove from the heat. Transfer to a paper towel to cool and crisp up.

3. Turn off the slow cooker. Taste and adjust the seasoning, if needed.

4. In a medium skillet, warm the chicken over medium-low heat. Divide the soup among serving bowls.

5. Top each bowl with the chicken, scallions, hard-boiled eggs, and garlic chips.

Flavor Tip: Heat the rice in the slow cooker on high with the canola oil, ginger, and minced garlic with the lid off, stirring occasionally, for 15 minutes, or until the rice is well coated with the oil, before adding the remaining ingredients.

Per Serving: Calories: 517; Total Fat: 20g; Saturated Fat: 4g; Carbohydrates: 52g; Sodium: 756mg; Fiber: 2g; Protein: 29g

Chicken Pho

DAIRY-FREE · EGG-FREE · GLUTEN-FREE · NUT-FREE

Serves 6

Prep time: 10 minutes / Cook time: 8 to 10 hours

Takeout—especially from Asian restaurants—is my go-to when I'm too busy to make dinner. But this tasty soup is a cinch to make and simmers all day without any attention. The only real work is in slicing up the fresh herbs and scallions to garnish it.

1 (3- to 4-pound) whole chicken
1 yellow onion, quartered
1 (2-inch) piece fresh ginger, halved and gently crushed with the broad side of a knife
2 cinnamon sticks
4 star anise
1 lemongrass stalk, halved
1 tablespoon fish sauce
12 cups water

Sea salt
Freshly ground black pepper
8 ounces wide rice noodles, soaked in hot water for 15 minutes before serving
1 cup fresh cilantro, for serving
Handful fresh basil or Thai basil leaves, for serving

Handful fresh mint leaves, for serving
2 scallions, white and green parts, thinly sliced on a bias, for serving
1 cup bean sprouts, for serving
2 limes, cut into wedges, for serving

1. Put the chicken, onion, ginger, cinnamon, star anise, lemongrass, fish sauce, and water in the slow cooker. Season generously with salt. Stir, then cover and cook on low for 8 to 10 hours.

2. Turn off the slow cooker. Remove the chicken, and place on a cutting board. When cool enough to handle, use two forks to shred the meat. Save the bones for another use.

3. Use a wire-mesh sieve to strain the broth. Discard the aromatics. Taste and adjust the seasoning, if needed.

4. Divide the soaked rice noodles among serving bowls. Ladle a generous amount of broth into each bowl. Top with some of the shredded chicken, cilantro, basil, mint, scallions, and bean sprouts. Serve with the lime wedges.

Tip: To get more of the authentic phở flavor, char the onion before adding it to the slow cooker. Heat a medium cast-iron skillet over medium-high heat until very hot. Sear the onion, cut-side down, for about 5 to 7 minutes, or until just blackened.

Per Serving: Calories: 277; Total Fat: 3g; Saturated Fat: 1g; Carbohydrates: 35g; Sodium: 388mg; Fiber: 2g; Protein: 25g

Tender Pork Posole

DAIRY-FREE • EGG-FREE • GLUTEN-FREE • NUT-FREE

Serves 6

Prep time: 10 minutes / Cook time: 8 to 10 hours,
plus 5 minutes to warm the hominy

In this pork posole, boneless pork shoulder simmers all day in homemade chicken broth infused with onions, garlic, and chili powder. Only the pork cooks in the slow cooker, while the hominy waits on the side until you're just ready to serve. That's the beauty of slow-cooking—you can let things that take a long time to cook simmer all day without any effort, then stir in the quick-cooking ingredients at the end. Don't skimp on the toppings. They really make the dish.

2 tablespoons
   chili powder
1 teaspoon ground cumin
¼ teaspoon sea salt
¼ teaspoon freshly
   ground black pepper
1½ pounds boneless pork
   shoulder, trimmed and
   cut into 4-inch pieces

2 yellow onions,
   diced, divided
5 garlic cloves, minced
8 cups Chicken
   Broth (page 17)
   or store-bought
1 (28-ounce) can hominy,
   drained and rinsed

½ bunch fresh cilantro,
   minced, for serving
1 bunch radishes, thinly
   sliced, for serving
2 ripe avocados, peeled,
   pitted, and diced,
   for serving
2 limes, cut into wedges,
   for serving

1. To make the rub, in a small bowl, combine the chili powder, cumin, salt, and pepper.

2. Coat the pork with the rub, and put it in the slow cooker.

3. Add half of the onions, the garlic, and the broth. Stir, then cover and cook on low for 8 to 10 hours.

4. Turn off the slow cooker. Stir in the hominy, and let it warm in the broth for 5 minutes before serving.

5. In a small bowl, combine the remaining onions with the cilantro.

6. Divide the soup among serving bowls. Top with the radishes, the onion-and-cilantro mixture, and avocados. Serve with the lime wedges.

✳ **Flavor Tip:** For even more flavor, season the pork on all sides with spice rub, and then heat a large skillet over medium-high heat. Pour in just enough canola oil to coat the bottom. Sear the pork on all sides for about 10 minutes, or until well browned.

Per Serving: Calories: 453; Total Fat: 16g; Saturated Fat: 8g; Carbohydrates: 48g; Sodium: 687mg; Fiber: 16g; Protein: 32g

Italian Wedding Soup

NUT-FREE

Serves 6

Prep time: 10 minutes / Cook time: 8 hours, plus 10 minutes to cook the pasta

I make no claims to the authenticity of this version of Italian wedding soup. It takes one tremendous shortcut and uses frozen meatballs. Gasp! I know, it's not traditional. But neither is spending five minutes to make dinner while you race out the door for work, sit in traffic, and then endure back-to-back meetings. So, give yourself a break and let frozen food and your trusty slow cooker handle dinner.

1 (2-pound) bag frozen Italian meatballs, thawed in the refrigerator overnight

1 pound escarole or endive, coarsely chopped

2 carrots, diced

1 celery stalk, diced

1 small yellow onion, diced

12 cups Chicken Broth (page 17) or store-bought

Sea salt

Freshly ground black pepper

1 cup orzo

2 large eggs

2 ounces parmesan cheese, grated with a Microplane

1. Put the meatballs, escarole, carrots, celery, onion, and broth in the slow cooker. Stir, then cover and cook on low for 8 hours.

2. Taste and adjust the seasoning, if needed.

3. Add the orzo, cover again, and cook for 10 minutes, or until al dente.

4. In a small bowl, whisk together the eggs and cheese. Stir the soup around in a circle. Slowly drizzle in the egg and cheese mixture so that it cooks and forms thin strands as you go.

5. Turn off the slow cooker. Taste the soup again, and adjust the seasoning, if needed. Divide among serving bowls.

Variation Tip: If escarole isn't your thing, use baby spinach. Don't add it until after the egg and parmesan mixture, and allow it to wilt about 1 minute before serving.

Per Serving: Calories: 584; Total Fat: 38g; Saturated Fat: 14g; Carbohydrates: 32g; Sodium: 1233mg; Fiber: 7g; Protein: 30g

Persian Lamb and Rice Soup

DAIRY-FREE • EGG-FREE • GLUTEN-FREE • NUT-FREE

Serves 6

Prep time: 10 minutes / Cook time: 8 to 10 hours

In this comforting soup, the flavors of onions, parsley, and fragrant spices infuse brown rice and split peas as they soften into oblivion, creating a luxurious base for the lamb shoulder. If you can get your hands on pomegranate molasses, it provides a tangy contrast to the herbaceous soup. It can be found in Middle Eastern markets or occasionally in the international foods section of the grocery store.

1 pound lamb shoulder, cut into 1-inch pieces

1 cup thinly sliced (from stem to roots) red onions

1 cup minced fresh flat-leaf parsley

1 cup brown rice

1 cup dried green split peas

½ cup coarsely chopped dried apricots

¼ teaspoon ground cinnamon

½ teaspoon ground turmeric

12 cups Chicken Broth (page 17) or store-bought

½ cup minced fresh mint

½ cup minced fresh cilantro

Sea salt

Freshly ground black pepper

Pomegranate molasses, for serving (optional)

1. Put the lamb, onions, parsley, rice, peas, apricots, cinnamon, turmeric, and broth in the slow cooker. Stir, then cover and cook on low for 8 to 10 hours.

2. Turn off the slow cooker. Stir in the mint and cilantro. Taste and adjust the seasoning, if needed. Divide among serving bowls.

3. Drizzle each bowl with pomegranate molasses (if using).

❋ **Substitution Tip:** Don't try to use regular molasses. If you can't find pomegranate molasses, give balsamic reduction (sometimes called balsamic glaze) a try. To make it, place 1 cup good balsamic vinegar into a small heavy-bottomed saucepan and simmer over low heat until reduced to about ⅓ cup. Be careful, it is very fragrant and burns easily.

Per Serving: Calories: 385; Total Fat: 8g; Saturated Fat: 3g; Carbohydrates: 54g; Sodium: 170mg; Fiber: 11g; Protein: 26g

Beef and Barley Soup

DAIRY-FREE • EGG-FREE • NUT-FREE

Serves 6 to 8

Prep time: 15 minutes / Cook time: 8 hours

One of my earliest memories of slow cooker meals was a beef stew my mom made when I was about five. Ignoring the advice of my parents, my little brother "seasoned" his with copious amounts of black pepper. Needless to say, he didn't finish his meal. If you're serving this to little ones, reserve the black pepper for serving . . . and maybe consider keeping it out of reach!

1½ pounds beef chuck, cut into 2-inch pieces

1 pound Yukon gold potatoes, quartered

4 carrots, diced

1 yellow onion, diced

2 celery stalks, minced

¾ cup pearl barley

3 garlic cloves, minced

1 tablespoon tomato paste

1 teaspoon minced fresh thyme

½ teaspoon sea salt, plus more as needed

½ teaspoon freshly ground black pepper, plus more as needed

8 cups Beef Stock (page 18) or store-bought

1. Put the beef, potatoes, carrots, onion, celery, barley, garlic, tomato paste, thyme, salt, pepper, and stock in the slow cooker. Stir; then cover and cook on low for 8 hours.

2. Turn off the slow cooker. Taste and adjust the seasoning, if needed. Divide the soup among serving bowls.

   * **Flavor Tip:** For maximum flavor, brown the meat before adding it to the slow cooker. Heat a large skillet over medium-high heat. Pat the beef dry with paper towels. Pour in just enough canola oil to coat the bottom of the skillet. Sear the beef in batches, to avoid crowding the skillet, for about 10 minutes per batch, or until it is well browned on all sides. Proceed with the recipe as directed.

Per Serving: Calories: 327; Total Fat: 7g; Saturated Fat: 2g; Carbohydrates: 39g; Sodium: 333mg; Fiber: 7g; Protein: 28g

Beef Chuck Chili
page 95

CHAPTER 6

Chowders and Chilis

Chicken and Corn Chowder 84

   BONUS: Buttermilk Corn Bread 85

Three-Bean Vegan Chili 86

Tandoori Chicken Chowder 87

White Chicken Chili 88

Chicken and Sausage Gumbo 90

Chipotle Turkey Chili 92

Pork Chili Verde 94

Beef Chuck Chili 95

Seafood Chowder 96

Chicken and Corn Chowder

EGG-FREE • GLUTEN-FREE • NUT-FREE

Serves 6

Prep time: 5 minutes / Cook time: 8 to 10 hours

Old Bay seasoning gives this creamy, sweet corn and chicken chowder a little kick. Keep the corn theme going, and serve with a tender Buttermilk Corn Bread (recipe follows).

4 ears corn, kernels removed with a knife, cobs reserved, divided

2 bone-in chicken leg quarters, skinned

2 cups diced peeled potatoes

1 cup minced yellow onion

1 leek, thinly sliced (see tip)

1 celery stalk, minced

2 garlic cloves, minced

2 fresh thyme sprigs

1 tablespoon Old Bay seasoning

8 cups Chicken Broth (page 17) or store-bought

½ cup heavy cream

Sea salt

Freshly ground black pepper

1. Break the corn cobs in half. Reserve 2 cups of corn kernels, and place in a covered container in the refrigerator.

2. Put the corn cobs, remaining corn kernels, the chicken, potatoes, onion, leek, celery, garlic, thyme, Old Bay, and broth in the slow cooker. Stir, then cover and cook on low for 8 to 10 hours.

3. Turn off the slow cooker. Remove the chicken, and place on a cutting board. When cool enough to handle, use two forks to shred the meat. Save the bones for another use. Return the meat to the slow cooker.

4. Add the reserved corn kernels and heavy cream. Mix well. Taste and adjust the seasoning, if needed. Remove and discard the thyme sprigs. Divide the chowder among serving bowls.

* **Variation Tip:** Give this soup a Southwestern flair by swapping out the Old Bay for one 4-ounce can of green chiles and 1 tablespoon of smoked paprika.

Per Serving: Calories: 317; Total Fat: 12g; Saturated Fat: 6g; Carbohydrates: 32g; Sodium: 216mg; Fiber: 5g; Protein: 22g

Buttermilk Corn Bread

NUT-FREE • VEGETARIAN

Serves 6

Prep time: 10 minutes / Cook time: 20 to 25 minutes, plus 15 minutes to cool

1½ cups cornmeal

¾ cup all-
purpose flour

3 tablespoons
granulated sugar

1 teaspoon
baking powder

1 teaspoon sea salt

1 large egg, beaten

2 tablespoons
butter, melted

1 cup buttermilk

1. Preheat the oven to 400°F. Line an 8-by-8-inch baking dish with parchment paper.

2. In a medium bowl, stir together the cornmeal, flour, sugar, baking powder, and salt. Make a well in the center.

3. Add the egg, butter, and buttermilk to the well. Stir until just incorporated and no lumps remain. Don't overmix.

4. Pour the mixture into the prepared dish, transfer to the oven, and bake for 20 to 22 minutes, or until a toothpick comes out clean when inserted into the center of the bread. Remove from the oven. Let cool for at least 15 minutes before serving.

* **Substitution Tip:** A gluten-free flour blend such as Cup4Cup or Bob's Red Mill 1 to 1 works well in this recipe.

Per Serving: Calories: 288; Total Fat: 6g; Saturated Fat: 3g; Carbohydrates: 52g; Sodium: 410mg; Fiber: 2g; Protein: 7g

Three-Bean Vegan Chili

DAIRY-FREE · EGG-FREE · GLUTEN-FREE · NUT-FREE · VEGAN

Serves 6

Prep time: 5 minutes / Cook time: 8 to 10 hours

Kidney beans, pinto beans, and black beans bring loads of protein to this vegan chili. Mushrooms add a savory, umami flavor, so you won't even miss the meat. The recipe calls for "good-quality" chili powder. That means choose a brand that has good reviews and, ideally, is organic. It really does make a difference. To keep it plant-based, serve with lots of shredded vegan cheese, dairy-free sour cream, and diced avocado.

2 (15-ounce) cans chili beans, mild or hot

1 (28-ounce) can diced fire-roasted tomatoes

1 (15-ounce) can black beans, drained

1 (15-ounce) can kidney beans, drained

2 cups cremini mushrooms, finely chopped

1 yellow onion, diced

2 carrots, diced

2 celery stalks, diced

6 garlic cloves, minced

1 serrano pepper, cored and minced

2 tablespoons good-quality chili powder

1 tablespoon ground cumin

1 teaspoon sea salt

1 teaspoon freshly ground black pepper

¼ teaspoon ground cinnamon

1. Put the chili beans, tomatoes, black beans, kidney beans, mushrooms, onion, carrots, celery, garlic, serrano pepper, chili powder, cumin, salt, pepper, and cinnamon in the slow cooker. Stir, then cover and cook on low for 8 to 10 hours.

2. Turn off the slow cooker. Divide the chili among serving bowls.

* **Flavor Tip:** For more flavor, heat a large skillet over high heat, and add just enough canola oil to coat the bottom. Sear the mushrooms in batches, being careful not to crowd the skillet, for about 3 minutes per batch, or until the mushrooms are well browned.

Per Serving: Calories: 301; Total Fat: 2g; Saturated Fat: 0g; Carbohydrates: 57g; Sodium: 640mg; Fiber: 21g; Protein: 18g

Tandoori Chicken Chowder

EGG-FREE · GLUTEN-FREE · NUT-FREE

Serves 6

Prep time: 5 minutes / Cook time: 8 hours

This chowder captures all of the flavors of tandoori chicken. Fragrant garam masala, turmeric, and ginger permeate a thick stew of potatoes, onion, and peas.

1 pound Yukon gold potatoes, cut into 1-inch pieces

1 pound boneless skinless chicken thighs, cut into 2-inch pieces

1 red onion, halved and thinly sliced from stem to roots

1 tablespoon minced fresh ginger

2 teaspoons minced garlic

1 tablespoon garam masala

1 teaspoon ground turmeric

½ teaspoon sea salt, plus more as needed

½ teaspoon freshly ground black pepper, plus more as needed

8 cups Chicken Broth (page 17) or store-bought

1 cup full-fat plain Greek yogurt

1 cup frozen peas, thawed

½ cup coarsely chopped fresh mint, for serving

1. Put the potatoes, chicken, onion, ginger, garlic, garam masala, turmeric, salt, pepper, and broth in the slow cooker. Stir, then cover and cook on low for 8 hours.

2. Turn off the slow cooker. Stir in the yogurt and peas. Taste and adjust the seasoning, if needed. Divide the chowder among serving bowls.

3. Top each bowl with mint.

Per Serving: Calories: 196; Total Fat: 5g; Saturated Fat: 2g; Carbohydrates: 19g; Sodium: 391mg; Fiber: 3g; Protein: 19g

White Chicken Chili

Serves 6

Prep time: 5 minutes / Cook time: 8 to 10 hours

Sometimes you want the hearty texture of a chili without the intensity of tomato and ground beef. This chicken chili is a subtle but flavorful version that will answer your cravings. Serve it with plenty of fresh avocado, minced cilantro, and tortilla chips.

2 bone-in chicken leg quarters, skinned

2 (4-ounce) cans green chiles

1 yellow onion, diced

6 garlic cloves, minced

2 (15-ounce) cans white beans

1 tablespoon ground cumin

1 teaspoon chili powder

8 cups Chicken Broth (page 17) or store-bought

8 ounces cream cheese

Sea salt

Freshly ground black pepper

1 to 2 tablespoons freshly squeezed lime juice

Peeled, pitted, and diced ripe avocado, for serving

Minced fresh cilantro, for serving

Tortilla chips, for serving

1. Put the chicken, chiles, onion, garlic, beans, cumin, chili powder, and broth in the slow cooker. Stir, then cover and cook on low for 8 to 10 hours.

2. Turn off the slow cooker. Remove the chicken, and place on a cutting board.

3. While the chicken cools, stir the cream cheese into the chili, cover, let soften completely, and then stir.

4. When the chicken is cool enough to handle, use two forks to shred the meat. Save the bones for another use. Return the meat to the slow cooker. Taste and adjust the seasoning, if needed.

5. Drizzle in just enough lime juice to balance the richness of the cream cheese. Divide the soup among serving bowls.

6. Top each bowl with avocado, cilantro, and tortilla chips.

Substitution Tip: If you prefer to use fresh chiles, use 1 jalapeño pepper (mild), seeded and finely chopped, or 1 serrano pepper (spicier) and 2 poblano peppers, seeded and finely chopped.

Per Serving: Calories: 439; Total Fat: 22g; Saturated Fat: 9g; Carbohydrates: 32g; Sodium: 345mg; Fiber: 9g; Protein: 30g

Chicken and Sausage Gumbo

EGG-FREE • NUT-FREE

Serves 6

Prep time: 10 minutes / Cook time: 8 hours, plus 15 minutes to make the roux

Traditional gumbo is thickened with a roux, a mixture of butter and flour that has been cooked over low heat until golden brown, or sometimes darker. It imparts a rich flavor to the gumbo, so if you have the time, invest about 15 minutes to make it before starting the slow cooker time. If you don't have the time, just add the butter and flour directly to the slow cooker.

3 tablespoons butter

3 tablespoons all-purpose flour

1 cup long-grain brown rice

1 green bell pepper, diced

2 celery stalks, diced

1 onion, diced

8 ounces okra, sliced

1 tablespoon fresh thyme leaves

1 teaspoon dried oregano

¼ teaspoon cayenne

1 (15-ounce) can fire-roasted diced tomatoes

4 cups Chicken Broth (page 17) or store-bought

4 boneless skinless chicken thighs, cut into 2-inch pieces

1 pound andouille sausage, cut into ½-inch pieces

Sea salt

Freshly ground black pepper

Fresh flat-leaf parsley, for serving

2 lemons, cut into wedges, for serving

1. To make the roux, in a small skillet, combine the butter and flour, and cook over low heat, whisking frequently, for about 15 minutes, or until it is golden brown and has a delicious nutty smell.

2. Put the rice, bell pepper, celery, onion, okra, thyme, oregano, cayenne, and roux in the slow cooker along with the tomatoes and broth. Stir, then add the chicken and sausage. Stir again, then cover and cook on low for 8 hours.

3. Turn off the slow cooker. Taste and adjust the seasoning, if needed. Divide the gumbo among serving bowls.

4. Serve the gumbo with fresh flat-leaf parsley and the lemon wedges.

Substitution Tip: Okra lacks popularity outside the South, so if you'd rather, dice 1 medium zucchini and use that instead. It softens and thickens the stew as well, but may be a little more approachable.

Per Serving: Calories: 614; Total Fat: 34g; Saturated Fat: 13g; Carbohydrates: 40g; Sodium: 849mg; Fiber: 5g; Protein: 39g

Chipotle Turkey Chili

DAIRY-FREE • EGG-FREE • GLUTEN-FREE • NUT-FREE

Serves 6

Prep time: 15 minutes / Cook time: 8 to 10 hours,
plus 10 minutes to cook the ground turkey

Turkey is leaner than ground beef, which is good from a health perspective. It's also milder in flavor, so it needs a more generous dose of spices. Chipotle peppers in adobo sauce do the trick. The acid from the adobo sauce coupled with the heat and smokiness from the chiles brings a nice complexity to this chili. The adobo sauce is pretty spicy, so I provide a range of measurements depending on how hot you like it.

1 tablespoon canola oil, divided

2 pounds ground turkey, divided

2 (15-ounce) cans pinto beans, drained

1 (15-ounce) can fire-roasted diced tomatoes

1 (12-ounce) jar fire-roasted red peppers, drained and finely chopped

1 cup diced peeled sweet potatoes

1 yellow onion, minced

6 garlic cloves, minced

1 chipotle in adobo sauce, minced, plus

1 to 3 teaspoons adobo sauce

1 tablespoon ground cumin

1 tablespoon chili powder

1 tablespoon smoked paprika

1 teaspoon sea salt

1 teaspoon freshly ground black pepper

1. Heat a large skillet over high heat.

2. Pour in ½ tablespoon of oil, and tilt to coat the skillet.

3. Add about 1 pound of turkey, and cook for about 5 minutes, or until just browned. Transfer to the slow cooker. Repeat with the remaining ½ tablespoon of oil and 1 pound of turkey. Remove from the heat.

4. Add the beans, tomatoes, peppers, sweet potatoes, onion, garlic, chipotle and adobo sauce, cumin, chili powder, paprika, salt, and pepper to the slow cooker. Stir, then cover and cook on low for 8 to 10 hours.

5. Turn off the slow cooker. Divide the chili among serving bowls.

Variation Tip: If you're short on time, you can skip steps 1 through 3 and simply break the turkey up into pieces before adding to the slow cooker. But the turkey has better flavor and texture if browned first.

Per Serving: Calories: 432; Total Fat: 15g; Saturated Fat: 3g; Carbohydrates: 36g; Sodium: 677mg; Fiber: 12g; Protein: 40g

Pork Chili Verde

EGG-FREE · GLUTEN-FREE · NUT-FREE

Serves 6

Prep time: 5 minutes / Cook time: 8 to 10 hours

Tender pork simmers all day in a tangy salsa verde and savory chicken broth in this easy chili recipe. Mexican salsa verde is typically made with a blend of toma-tillos, which contain pectin and add body to the chili, and green chiles. Instead of traditional beans, I opt for chickpeas, which tend to hold their shape better during long cooking times.

1 teaspoon onion powder
1 teaspoon garlic powder
1 teaspoon
  smoked paprika
1 tablespoon ancho
  chile powder
1 teaspoon sea salt
1 teaspoon freshly
  ground black pepper

1½ pounds pork shoulder
1 yellow onion, diced
6 garlic cloves, minced
2 (15-ounce) can
  chickpeas, drained
2 (14-ounce) jars
  salsa verde

8 cups Chicken
  Broth (page 17)
  or store-bought
Shredded white Cheddar
  cheese, for serving
Sour cream, for serving

1. To make the spice rub, in a small bowl, combine the onion powder, garlic powder, smoked paprika, ancho chile powder, salt, and pepper.
2. Coat the pork with the spice rub, then put it in the slow cooker.
3. Add the onion, garlic, chickpeas, salsa, and broth. Stir, then cover and cook on low for 8 to 10 hours.
4. Turn off the slow cooker. Divide the chili among serving bowls.
5. Top each bowl with cheese and sour cream.

  ❈ **Time-Saving Prep Tip:** To really infuse the pork with flavor, coat it in the spice blend a day ahead of time, cover with plastic wrap, and refrigerate overnight.

Per Serving: Calories: 480; Total Fat: 21g; Saturated Fat: 8g; Carbohydrates: 36g; Sodium: 1289mg; Fiber: 7g; Protein: 34g

Beef Chuck Chili

EGG-FREE ● GLUTEN-FREE ● NUT-FREE

Serves 6

Prep time: 10 minutes / Cook time: 8 to 10 hours

Often beef chili is made with ground beef. That's handy when you want a meal on the table in less than an hour. But if you want less work and are willing to wait, the slow cooker transforms beef chuck into tender bites of beef. Any other beef stew meat is fine, too.

2 pounds beef chuck, cut into 1-inch pieces
1 yellow onion, diced
2 carrots, diced
2 celery stalks, diced
1 green bell pepper, diced
4 garlic cloves, minced
1 (28-ounce) can fire-roasted tomatoes

1 (15-ounce) can kidney beans, drained and rinsed
1 tablespoon ancho chile powder
1 tablespoon smoked paprika
1 tablespoon ground cumin

1 teaspoon sea salt
1 teaspoon freshly ground black pepper
Sour cream, for serving
Coarsely chopped fresh cilantro, for serving
Shredded white Cheddar cheese, for serving

1. Put the beef, onion, carrots, celery, bell pepper, garlic, tomatoes, beans, ancho chile powder, paprika, cumin, salt, and pepper in the slow cooker. Stir, then cover and cook on low for 8 to 10 hours.

2. Turn off the slow cooker. Divide the chili among serving bowls.

3. Top each bowl with sour cream, cilantro, and cheese.

Flavor Tip: For maximum flavor, brown the meat before adding it to the slow cooker: Heat a large skillet over medium-high heat. Pat the beef dry with paper towels. Pour in just enough canola oil to coat the bottom of the skillet. Sear the beef in batches, to avoid crowding the skillet, for about 15 minutes, or until well browned on all sides. Proceed with the recipe as directed.

Per Serving: Calories: 426; Total Fat: 20g; Saturated Fat: 8g; Carbohydrates: 23g; Sodium: 861mg; Fiber: 8g; Protein: 42g

Seafood Chowder

EGG-FREE • GLUTEN-FREE • NUT-FREE

Serves 6

Prep time: 15 minutes / Cook time: 8 hours, plus 10 minutes to cook the seafood

One of my earliest memories is of my mom taking me out on our boat to hook "the one that got away." We got caught in a huge storm and left the water empty-handed. Other adventures were more successful, and we found many tasty ways to prepare fresh fish and shellfish. Here's my take on my mom's seafood chowder.

1 pound Yukon gold potatoes, diced
1 yellow onion, diced
2 celery stalks, diced
¼ cup minced fresh flat-leaf parsley

1 teaspoon fresh thyme leaves
¼ teaspoon red pepper flakes
8 cups Fish Stock (page 19) or store-bought

1 pound fresh salmon fillets
1 pound mussels
8 ounces bay scallops
1 cup heavy cream

1. Put the potatoes, onion, celery, parsley, thyme, red pepper flakes, and fish stock in the slow cooker. Stir, then cover and cook on low for 8 hours.

2. Cut the salmon into 2-inch pieces, and scrub and debeard the mussels.

3. Remove 2 cups of soup to a blender, vent the lid, cover with a kitchen towel, and blend until smooth. Return the puree to the slow cooker, and mix well.

4. Add the salmon, mussels, scallops, and heavy cream. Cover, and continue cooking for 8 to 10 minutes, or until the salmon has cooked through and all of the mussels have opened. Discard any mussels that fail to open after 10 minutes.

5. Turn off the slow cooker. Divide the chowder among serving bowls.

 * **Substitution Tip:** You can swap out the salmon for another firm-fleshed fish, such as halibut. You can also swap out the mussels for clams.

Per Serving: Calories: 403; Total Fat: 21g; Saturated Fat: 10g; Carbohydrates: 20g; Sodium: 424mg; Fiber: 2g; Protein: 31g

Beef Bourguignon
page 120

CHAPTER 7

Stews

Peanut Stew with Collard Greens 100

Creamy White Bean and Wheat Berry Stew 101

Coq au Vin Blanc 102

Mediterranean Chicken Stew 103

Cuban Chicken Stew 104

Pollo en Escabeche 105

Chicken Adobo Stew 106

Chicken Afritada Stew 107

Jamaican Jerk Chicken Stew 108

   BONUS: Tropical Fruit Salad 109

Coconut-Curry Chicken Stew 110

Panang Duck Curry with Pineapple 111

Ham and White Bean Stew 112

Polenta and Pork Stew 113

   BONUS: Red Cabbage Slaw 115

Moroccan Lamb Stew 116

Mediterranean Seafood Stew 117

Miso Beef Stew 118

Chinese Beef Stew 119

Beef Bourguignon 120

Peanut Stew with Collard Greens

DAIRY-FREE • EGG-FREE • VEGAN

Serves 4

Prep time: 5 minutes / Cook time: 6 to 8 hours

How many amazing recipes begin with onion, garlic, and ginger? Some of my favorite chefs—Melissa Clark, Alison Roman, and Sarah Britton—build some of their best recipes off this trio. You might think that all end up having a similar flavor, but that's not the case at all. In this recipe, this trio serves as a base for Southeast Asian flavors. Think of it as if your favorite peanut sauce became a stew.

1 cup peanut butter
¼ cup low-sodium
  soy sauce
½ cup tomato paste
8 cups Essential
  Vegetable Broth
  (page 14) or store-
  bought, divided

1 bunch collard greens,
  thinly sliced
1 yellow onion, minced
4 garlic cloves, minced

1 tablespoon minced
  fresh ginger
1 teaspoon sea salt
¼ teaspoon cayenne

1. In a medium bowl, whisk together the peanut butter, soy sauce, tomato paste, and ½ cup of broth until slightly thinned. Pour into the slow cooker.

2. Add the remaining 7½ cups of broth, the collard greens, onion, garlic, ginger, salt, and cayenne. Stir, then cover and cook on low for 6 to 8 hours.

3. Turn off the slow cooker. Divide the stew among serving bowls.

* **Substitution Tip:** Almond butter works just as well as peanut butter in this recipe. In fact, that is how I made the soup the first several times I tried it.

Per Serving: Calories: 453; Total Fat: 34g; Saturated Fat: 7g; Carbohydrates: 28g; Sodium: 1453mg; Fiber: 7g; Protein: 19g

Creamy White Bean and Wheat Berry Stew

EGG-FREE • NUT-FREE • VEGETARIAN

Serves 6

Prep time: 5 minutes / Cook time: 8 to 10 hours

Creamy, smoky, and hearty, this vegetarian stew has it all. Protein-rich cannellini beans and wheat berries simmer in a flavorful broth. The smokiness of the paprika and fire-roasted tomatoes is softened by a generous splash of heavy cream.

2 (15-ounce) cans cannellini beans, drained and rinsed

1 cup wheat berries

1 yellow onion, halved and thinly sliced from stem to roots

1 tablespoon smoked paprika

1 (15-ounce) can fire-roasted diced tomatoes

4 cups Essential Vegetable Broth (page 14) or store-bought

½ cup heavy cream

½ cup coarsely chopped fresh flat-leaf parsley

½ cup coarsely chopped fresh basil

1. Put the beans, wheat berries, onion, paprika, tomatoes, and broth in the slow cooker. Stir, then cover and cook on low for 8 to 10 hours.

2. Turn off the slow cooker. Stir in the heavy cream, parsley, and basil. Divide the stew among serving bowls.

Substitution Tip: To make a vegan version of this stew, swap out the heavy cream for 1 (15-ounce) can full-fat coconut milk, which can be added with the other ingredients in step 1.

Per Serving: Calories: 315; Total Fat: 9g; Saturated Fat: 5g; Carbohydrates: 50g; Sodium: 157mg; Fiber: 12g; Protein: 13g

Coq au Vin Blanc

EGG-FREE • GLUTEN-FREE • NUT-FREE

Serves 4 to 6

Prep time: 10 minutes / Cook time: 8 to 10 hours

Coq au vin, like many other French recipes, transforms everyday cuts of meat and vegetables into a five-star meal. The secret is in cooking with wine. It tenderizes meat and imbues it with flavor. I have had coq au vin made with red wine, but purple chicken looks strange to me. So, I opt for white wine. Do as you please though. The recipe will work fine with either wine.

2½ pounds bone-in chicken leg quarters, skinned

2 leeks, trimmed, washed, and thinly sliced (see tip)

1 yellow onion, halved and thinly sliced from stem to roots

8 ounces oyster mushrooms, coarsely chopped

8 garlic cloves, smashed

2 tablespoons butter

1 tablespoon minced fresh thyme

½ teaspoon sea salt

½ teaspoon freshly ground black pepper

2 cups dry white wine

2 cups Chicken Broth (page 17) or store-bought

1. Put the chicken, leeks, onion, mushrooms, garlic, butter, thyme, salt, pepper, wine, and broth in the slow cooker. Stir, then cover and cook on low for 8 to 10 hours.

2. Turn off the slow cooker. Divide the stew among serving bowls.

   Time-Saving Prep Tip: To prepare the leeks, cut off the root ends and then slice in half lengthwise. Rinse the leeks under cool running water, peeling away the layers so the water fully cleans between them. You don't have to peel them apart, just enough to let the water remove any trapped dirt.

   Substitution Tip: Oyster mushrooms have a delicate flavor and chewy texture that work well in this stew. If you can't find them or don't want to pay their slightly higher price, button mushrooms will work just fine.

Per Serving: Calories: 488; Total Fat: 16g; Saturated Fat: 6g; Carbohydrates: 17g; Sodium: 581mg; Fiber: 3g; Protein: 46g

Mediterranean Chicken Stew

DAIRY-FREE • EGG-FREE • GLUTEN-FREE • NUT-FREE

Serves 6

Prep time: 10 minutes / Cook time: 8 to 10 hours

This flavorful stew is worth the wait. Like most stews, it's actually even better on the second day. Tender chicken thighs bathe in a hearty mixture of artichoke hearts, olives, onions, and bell pepper. Serve with crusty bread to sop up the delicious broth.

2 pounds boneless skinless chicken thighs, halved

1 (15-ounce) jar artichoke hearts, rinsed, drained, and halved

1 yellow onion, diced

4 ripe tomatoes, coarsely chopped

1 red bell pepper, cored and diced

8 garlic cloves, smashed

½ cup pitted Kalamata olives, sliced

2 tablespoons red-wine vinegar

1 tablespoon smoked paprika

Pinch red pepper flakes

4 cups Chicken Broth (page 17) or store-bought

1. Put the chicken, artichoke hearts, onion, tomatoes, bell pepper, garlic, olives, vinegar, paprika, red pepper flakes, and broth in the slow cooker. Stir, then cover and cook on low for 8 to 10 hours.

2. Turn off the slow cooker. Divide the stew among serving bowls.

❋ **Variation Tip:** This stew can also serve as a template for cooking a whole chicken. Remove the skin from a 3-pound bird, and season liberally with salt and pepper. Continue with the recipe as written. After cooking, slice the meat from the bird, and return it to the stew.

Per Serving: Calories: 267; Total Fat: 8g; Saturated Fat: 2g; Carbohydrates: 16g; Sodium: 301mg; Fiber: 6g; Protein: 34g

Cuban Chicken Stew

DAIRY-FREE • EGG-FREE • GLUTEN-FREE • NUT-FREE

Serves 6
Prep time: 5 minutes / Cook time: 8 hours

Bell pepper, dried oregano, capers, olives, and loads of citrus liven up a basic chicken-and-potato stew inspired by the flavors of Cuba. In this recipe, the chicken thighs are cooked and served with the bone in. If you prefer a more elegant presentation, you can remove the chicken and place it on a cutting board after cooking. When it is cool enough to handle, remove the meat in large chunks, add the meat back to the stew, and discard the bones.

1 lime

1 orange

2 pounds bone-in
  chicken thighs, skinned

1 pound Yukon gold
  potatoes, halved

1 green bell pepper,
  finely diced

1 yellow onion, diced

4 garlic cloves, smashed

½ cup
  pepper-stuffed olives

¼ cup raisins

3 tablespoons capers

2 teaspoons
  dried oregano

8 cups Chicken
  Broth (page 17)
  or store-bought

1 cup frozen
  peas, thawed

½ cup minced fresh
  flat-leaf parsley

Sea salt

Freshly ground
  black pepper

1. Zest and juice the lime and orange. Put the zest from both in the slow cooker. Add 1 tablespoon of lime juice and all of the orange juice to the slow cooker along with the chicken, potatoes, bell pepper, onion, garlic, olives, raisins, capers, oregano, and broth. Stir, then cover and cook on low for 8 hours.

2. Turn off the slow cooker. Stir in the peas, parsley, and remaining lime juice. Taste and adjust the seasoning, if needed. Divide the stew among serving bowls.

* **Flavor Tip:** I prefer to always use flat-leaf parsley, also known as Italian parsley. I find the texture more appealing and the flavor more pronounced.

Per Serving: Calories: 238; Total Fat: 6g; Saturated Fat: 1g; Carbohydrates: 20g; Sodium: 387mg; Fiber: 4g; Protein: 25g

Pollo en Escabeche

DAIRY-FREE ● EGG-FREE ● GLUTEN-FREE ● NUT-FREE

Serves 6

Prep time: 5 minutes / Cook time: 8 to 10 hours

"Escabeche" is loosely translated from Spanish into English as "marinade." But it really is all about vinegar. You may recognize verduras en escabeche as the pickled vegetables available at most authentic Mexican restaurants. Pollo en escabeche is similar. Chicken thighs cook in a blend of onions, garlic, bell pepper, spices, white-wine vinegar, and broth. The result is a mouthwatering stew with the perfect balance of salt and acid. If that still sounds unusual, think about your favorite potato chip, the one you just can't stop eating. That's what we're going for here.

- 2 pounds bone-in chicken leg quarters, skinned
- 2 yellow onions, halved and thinly sliced from stem to roots
- 1 green bell pepper, cored and thinly sliced
- 4 garlic cloves, minced
- ⅔ cup white-wine vinegar
- 2 bay leaves
- 1 teaspoon ground cumin
- 1 teaspoon smoked paprika
- 1 teaspoon freshly ground black pepper, plus more as needed
- ¼ teaspoon sea salt, plus more as needed
- 4 cups Chicken Broth (page 17) or store-bought

1. Put the chicken, onions, bell pepper, garlic, vinegar, bay leaves, cumin, paprika, pepper, salt, and broth in the slow cooker. Stir, then cover and cook on low for 8 to 10 hours.

2. Turn off the slow cooker. Remove the chicken, and place on a cutting board. When cool enough to handle, use two forks to shred the meat. Save the bones for another use. Return the meat to the slow cooker, and then stir. Taste and adjust the seasoning, if needed. Remove and discard the bay leaves. Divide the stew among serving bowls.

Per Serving: Calories: 166; Total Fat: 5g; Saturated Fat: 1g; Carbohydrates: 6g; Sodium: 267mg; Fiber: 1g; Protein: 23g

Chicken Adobo Stew

DAIRY-FREE ● EGG-FREE ● NUT-FREE

Serves 6
Prep time: 10 minutes / Cook time: 8 to 10 hours

Similar to pollo en escabeche, vinegar is the essential ingredient in chicken adobo. This version of the classic Filipino dish includes large chunks of carrots, green beans, shallots, and napa cabbage for a chunky stew. Serve over steamed white rice.

2 pounds boneless skinless chicken thighs, halved

4 medium carrots, cut into 2-inch pieces

½ head napa cabbage, cored and cut into 2-inch chunks

8 ounces green beans, trimmed

6 shallots, peeled and halved

4 garlic cloves, minced

½ cup low-sodium soy sauce

½ cup white vinegar

2 bay leaves

1 teaspoon freshly ground black pepper

4 cups Chicken Broth (page 17) or store-bought

½ bunch fresh cilantro, coarsely chopped, for serving

1. Put the chicken, carrots, cabbage, green beans, shallots, garlic, soy sauce, vinegar, bay leaves, pepper, and broth in the slow cooker. Stir, then cover and cook on low for 8 to 10 hours.

2. Turn off the slow cooker. Remove and discard the bay leaves. Divide the stew among serving bowls.

3. Top each bowl with cilantro.

* **Variation Tip:** Feel free to vary the vegetables according to what's in season. If you use leafy greens, wait to add them until the end of the cooking time. Just allow them to wilt, then serve.

Per Serving: Calories: 211; Total Fat: 5g; Saturated Fat: 1g; Carbohydrates: 15g; Sodium: 819mg; Fiber: 5g; Protein: 27g

Chicken Afritada Stew

DAIRY-FREE • EGG-FREE • NUT-FREE

Serves 6

Prep time: 10 minutes / Cook time: 8 hours

Afritada is a lesser-known Filipino dish that has a mild flavor built around savory vegetables and tomato sauce. Sometimes green peas and hot dogs are also added, but I kept this one simple.

2 pounds boneless skinless chicken thighs

1 pound Yukon gold potatoes, halved

1 yellow onion, diced

2 carrots, sliced

1 red bell pepper, cored and sliced

4 garlic cloves, minced

2 bay leaves

3 tablespoons fish sauce

1 tablespoon low-sodium soy sauce

1 tablespoon freshly squeezed lemon juice

1 teaspoon freshly ground black pepper

1 (15-ounce) can tomato sauce

6 cups Chicken Broth (page 17) or store-bought

1. Put the chicken, potatoes, onion, carrots, bell pepper, garlic, bay leaves, fish sauce, soy sauce, lemon juice, pepper, tomato sauce, and broth in the slow cooker. Stir, then cover and cook on low for 8 hours.

2. Turn off the slow cooker, and remove and discard the bay leaves. Divide the stew among serving bowls.

Per Serving: Calories: 244; Total Fat: 5g; Saturated Fat: 1g; Carbohydrates: 24g; Sodium: 726mg; Fiber: 4g; Protein: 26g

Jamaican Jerk Chicken Stew

DAIRY-FREE · EGG-FREE · GLUTEN-FREE · NUT-FREE

Serves 6

Prep time: 5 minutes / Cook time: 8 hours

The first time I made this jerk sauce, a heat wave had descended on Portland. It was unbearable. No one had air conditioning. Counterintuitively, the intense spice of the sauce was just what we needed. Cool things off with a sweet Tropical Fruit Salad (recipe follows).

1 red onion, diced

1 serrano pepper, cored and minced

2 garlic cloves, coarsely chopped

2 tablespoons molasses

2 teaspoons ground allspice

1 tablespoon minced fresh ginger

1 tablespoon freshly ground black pepper

2 teaspoons fresh thyme

1 teaspoon sea salt

¼ teaspoon ground cloves

6 cups Chicken Broth (page 17) or store-bought, divided

2 pounds bone-in chicken thighs, skinned

4 carrots, cut into ¼-inch pieces

4 shallots, peeled and sliced lengthwise

½ bunch cilantro, coarsely chopped, for serving

1. To make the sauce, put the onion, serrano pepper, garlic, molasses, allspice, ginger, pepper, thyme, salt, cloves, and 1 cup of chicken broth in a blender, and blend until smooth.

2. Pour the sauce into the slow cooker along with the remaining 5 cups of chicken broth, the chicken, carrots, and shallots. Stir, then cover and cook for 8 hours.

3. Turn off the slow cooker. The chicken can be served bone-in. Divide the stew among serving bowls.

4. Top each bowl with cilantro.

Per Serving: Calories: 190; Total Fat: 5g; Saturated Fat: 1g; Carbohydrates: 13g; Sodium: 529mg; Fiber: 2g; Protein: 23g

Tropical Fruit Salad

DAIRY-FREE • EGG-FREE • GLUTEN-FREE • NUT-FREE • VEGAN

Serves 6
Prep time: 10 minutes

2 tablespoons
  granulated sugar
3 tablespoons
  hot water
1 teaspoon freshly
  squeezed
  lime juice

¼ teaspoon
  ground cinnamon
⅛ teaspoon
  ground allspice
1 cantaloupe, seeded
  and cut into
  1-inch pieces

1 mango, pitted
  and cut into
  1-inch pieces
1 pineapple, cored
  and cut into
  1-inch pieces
Handful fresh mint,
  thinly sliced

1. In a large bowl, combine the sugar, water, lime juice, cinnamon, and allspice. Stir until the sugar has dissolved.

2. Add the cantaloupe, mango, and pineapple. Toss gently. Refrigerate until ready to serve.

3. Stir in the mint just before serving.

Per Serving: Calories: 109; Total Fat: 0g; Saturated Fat: 0g; Carbohydrates: 28g; Sodium: 2mg; Fiber: 3g; Protein: 1g

Coconut-Curry Chicken Stew

DAIRY-FREE • EGG-FREE • GLUTEN-FREE

Serves 6

Prep time: 10 minutes / Cook time: 8 hours

Store-bought green curry paste does the heavy lifting in this easy slow cooker stew. Sure, you could run to multiple stores to hunt down lemongrass, makrut lime leaves, and galangal. But sometimes you just need things to be easy, and this stew delivers. Serve with steamed jasmine rice.

2 pounds boneless skinless chicken thighs

8 ounces green beans, trimmed and cut into 2-inch pieces

1 yellow onion, halved and thinly sliced from stem to roots

2 plum tomatoes, cored and quartered

1 red bell pepper, cored and sliced

¼ cup green curry paste

3 tablespoons brown sugar

1 teaspoon sea salt

2 (14-ounce) cans full-fat coconut milk

2 cups Chicken Broth (page 17) or store-bought

2 tablespoons freshly squeezed lime juice

1. Put the chicken, green beans, onion, tomatoes, bell pepper, curry paste, brown sugar, salt, coconut milk, and broth in the slow cooker. Stir, then cover and cook on low for 8 hours.

2. Turn off the slow cooker. Stir in the lime juice. Divide the stew among serving bowls.

⁕ **Variation Tip:** Yellow or red curry paste will also work in this stew.

Per Serving: Calories: 459; Total Fat: 34g; Saturated Fat: 26g; Carbohydrates: 17g; Sodium: 521mg; Fiber: 4g; Protein: 27g

Panang Duck Curry with Pineapple

DAIRY-FREE • EGG-FREE • GLUTEN-FREE

Serves 6

Prep time: 5 minutes / Cook time: 8 hours

Whenever I'm in a Thai restaurant, panang curry is my go-to. Green beans, pineapple, peppers, and tender duck meat simmer in a spicy, creamy coconut broth. Like most Thai food, it has the perfect balance of salty, sweet, savory, and sour.

2 tablespoons panang curry paste

2 pounds bone-in duck legs, skinned

2 cups fresh or canned pineapple chunks, drained

8 ounces green beans, trimmed and cut into 2-inch pieces

2 tablespoons fish sauce

2 tablespoons brown sugar

1 tablespoon minced fresh ginger

1 tablespoon minced garlic

2 (14-ounce) cans coconut milk

1 to 2 tablespoons freshly squeezed lime juice

2 red bell peppers, cored and sliced

1 cup coarsely chopped fresh basil

1. Put the curry paste, duck, pineapple, green beans, fish sauce, sugar, ginger, garlic, and coconut milk in the slow cooker. Stir, then cover and cook on low for 8 hours.

2. Turn off the slow cooker. Add the lime juice, bell peppers, and basil. Remove the duck, and place on a cutting board. When cool enough to handle, remove the meat in large pieces. Save the bones for another use. Stir the meat back into the slow cooker. Divide the curry among serving bowls.

Flavor Tip: If you can find Thai basil in your supermarket or in an Asian market, use that instead of conventional basil in this dish.

Per Serving: Calories: 490; Total Fat: 36g; Saturated Fat: 28g; Carbohydrates: 22g; Sodium: 579mg; Fiber: 4g; Protein: 26g

Ham and White Bean Stew

DAIRY-FREE • EGG-FREE • GLUTEN-FREE • NUT-FREE

Serves 8

Prep time: 10 minutes / Cook time: 8 to 10 hours

With a bone-in ham and several cans of beans, this stew is designed for a crowd. It's a perfect one-pot winter meal after a long day playing in the snow. Fresh flat-leaf parsley, rosemary, and thyme bring so much flavor to the dish, so make sure to use fresh herbs. Often, you can find multiple herbs in one package.

1 (6- to 8-pound) bone-in half ham

4 (15-ounce) cans white beans, drained

4 celery stalks, minced

3 carrots, minced

2 yellow onions, diced

6 garlic cloves, smashed

½ cup minced fresh herbs, such as parsley, rosemary, and thyme

8 cups Chicken Broth (page 17) or store-bought

1. Put the ham, beans, celery, carrots, onions, garlic, herbs, and broth in the slow cooker. Stir, then cover and cook on low for 8 to 10 hours.

2. Turn off the slow cooker. Remove the ham, and place on a cutting board. When cool enough to handle, use two forks to shred the meat. Save the bones for another use. Return the meat to the slow cooker. Divide the stew among serving bowls.

* **Substitution Tip:** If you cannot find a bone-in ham, use a boneless ham and reduce the cooking time to 6 to 8 hours.

Per Serving: Calories: 378; Total Fat: 7g; Saturated Fat: 2g; Carbohydrates: 41g; Sodium: 1575mg; Fiber: 10g; Protein: 40g

Polenta and Pork Stew

DAIRY-FREE • EGG-FREE • GLUTEN-FREE • NUT-FREE

Serves 6

**Prep time: 15 minutes / Cook time: 8 to 10 hours,
plus 10 minutes to brown the pork**

Polenta thickens this cumin-scented pork stew, so there's no need for additional starch. A little extra prep work in this stew pays off in the long run. First, toast the ground cumin until it's fragrant. Then brown the pork in the same skillet before transferring to the slow cooker.

1 tablespoon
   ground cumin
2 pounds pork shoulder,
   cut into 2-inch pieces
Sea salt
Freshly ground
   black pepper
2 tablespoons canola oil

2 yellow onions, halved
   and thinly sliced from
   stem to roots
8 garlic cloves, smashed
½ cup polenta or
   fine cornmeal
8 cups Chicken
   Broth (page 17)
   or store-bought

2 ripe avocados, peeled,
   pitted, and diced,
   for serving
Warmed corn tortillas,
   for serving
Red Cabbage Slaw
   (recipe follows),
   for serving

1. Heat a large skillet over medium heat.

2. Put the cumin in the skillet, and toast for about 1 minute, or until fragrant. Do not burn. Transfer the cumin to the slow cooker, and carefully wipe the skillet clean.

3. Pat the pork shoulder dry with paper towels. Season generously with salt and pepper.

4. Pour the canola oil into the skillet, and tilt so the oil coats the bottom.

5. Add the pork, and brown on all sides for about 10 minutes, or until deep golden brown. You will likely need to do this in batches to avoid crowding the skillet. Remove from the heat. Transfer the pork to the slow cooker.

Continued

Polenta and Pork Stew continued

6. Add the onions, garlic, polenta, and broth to the slow cooker. Stir, then cover and cook on low for 8 to 10 hours.

7. Turn off the slow cooker. Divide the stew among serving bowls.

8. Serve the stew with the avocados, warmed corn tortillas, and red cabbage slaw.

Per Serving: Calories: 470; Total Fat: 24g; Saturated Fat: 5g; Carbohydrates: 31g; Sodium: 212mg; Fiber: 8g; Protein: 33g

Red Cabbage Slaw

DAIRY-FREE • EGG-FREE • GLUTEN-FREE • NUT-FREE • VEGAN

Serves 6
Prep time: 10 minutes

½ head red cabbage, cored and thinly sliced

½ red onion, thinly sliced from stem to roots

½ bunch fresh cilantro, coarsely chopped

2 tablespoons freshly squeezed lime juice

¼ teaspoon sea salt

In a large bowl, combine the cabbage, onion, cilantro, lime juice, and salt. Gently toss.

Per Serving: Calories: 24; Total Fat: 0g; Saturated Fat: 0g; Carbohydrates: 6g; Sodium: 117mg; Fiber: 2g; Protein: 1g

Moroccan Lamb Stew

DAIRY-FREE • EGG-FREE • GLUTEN-FREE

Serves 6 to 8

Prep time: 10 minutes / Cook time: 8 to 10 hours

Although the ingredient list is a little bit longer in this recipe than in others, each ingredient adds a layer of flavor. Apricots sweeten the dish, while onion, carrot, and celery form a base of flavor, and the spices add complexity. As with other meat stews, if you want to take the time to sear the lamb before adding it to the slow cooker, the browned meat will taste better. Serve with plenty of Indian naan or steamed jasmine rice. The dish is mild in terms of heat, but if you want a hotter dish, double the amount of cayenne.

2 pounds boneless lamb shoulder, cut into 1-inch pieces

1 yellow onion, halved and thinly sliced

1 carrot, diced

1 celery stalk, diced

½ cup sliced dried apricots

½ cup toasted slivered almonds

1 tablespoon minced fresh ginger

1 tablespoon ground cumin

1 tablespoon ground turmeric

1 teaspoon sea salt

1 teaspoon freshly ground black pepper

½ teaspoon ground allspice

½ teaspoon ground cinnamon

¼ teaspoon cayenne

6 cups Chicken Broth (page 17) or store-bought

1. Put the lamb, onion, carrot, celery, apricots, almonds, ginger, cumin, turmeric, salt, pepper, allspice, cinnamon, cayenne, and broth in the slow cooker. Stir, then cover and cook on low for 8 to 10 hours.

2. Turn off the slow cooker. Divide the stew among serving bowls.

* **Time-Saving Prep Tip:** Measure all of the spices ahead of time, and put them in a sealed container until you're ready to assemble the ingredients in the slow cooker.

Per Serving: Calories: 334; Total Fat: 17g; Saturated Fat: 6g; Carbohydrates: 14g; Sodium: 512mg; Fiber: 3g; Protein: 33g

Mediterranean Seafood Stew

Serves 4 to 6
Prep time: 10 minutes / Cook time: 8 to 10 hours,
plus 10 to 15 minutes to cook the seafood

This stew gives a strong nod to ratatouille, a Provençal dish of slow-cooked eggplant, zucchini, tomatoes, and herbs. The slow cooker makes for a perfect cooking vessel for it because it prevents the vegetables from scorching while allowing them to slowly meld into a nearly homogenous medley. The seafood cooks in a flash at the end. Serve with a loaf of crusty French bread.

¼ cup extra-virgin olive oil

1 red onion, halved and thinly sliced from stem to roots

4 garlic cloves, minced

1 eggplant, cut into 1-inch pieces

2 medium zucchini, cut into 1-inch pieces

1 (15-ounce) can plum tomatoes, hand torn

½ cup coarsely chopped fresh herbs, such as parsley, basil, thyme, and rosemary

Sea salt

Freshly ground black pepper

2 pounds clams

1 pound jumbo shrimp

1 lemon, cut into wedges

1. Put the oil, onion, garlic, eggplant, zucchini, tomatoes, and herbs in the slow cooker. Season generously with salt and pepper. Stir, then cover and cook on low for 8 to 10 hours.

2. Just before you're ready to serve, scrub the clams. Peel the shrimp. Nestle them into the vegetables, but don't completely bury them. Cover, increase the heat to high, and continue cooking for 10 to 15 minutes, or until the shrimp are opaque and the clams have opened. Discard any clams that have not opened after 15 minutes.

3. Turn off the slow cooker. Divide the stew among serving bowls.

4. Serve the stew with the lemon wedges.

Per Serving: Calories: 334; Total Fat: 15g; Saturated Fat: 2g; Carbohydrates: 21g; Sodium: 367mg; Fiber: 8g; Protein: 32g

Miso Beef Stew

DAIRY-FREE • EGG-FREE • NUT-FREE

Serves 6
Prep time: 5 minutes / Cook time: 8 to 10 hours

This stew is inspired by one of my favorite restaurants in LA—Lemonade. The restaurant has a healthy cafeteria vibe, but its red miso beef is absolutely decadent: fatty beef short ribs are simmered in a sticky sweet glaze of molasses and ketchup. My version swaps out the short ribs for beef chuck, which becomes just as tender after hours in the slow cooker. I also swap out the molasses and ketchup for tomato paste and just a couple tablespoons of brown sugar. I'm not going to call it a healthy food exactly, but it reins in some of the sugar and fat without sacrificing flavor.

2 pounds beef chuck, cut into 2-inch pieces
1 yellow onion, diced
4 garlic cloves, minced
½ cup red miso
¼ cup tomato paste

¼ cup apple cider vinegar
2 tablespoons brown sugar
1 tablespoon minced fresh ginger

1 tablespoon Dijon mustard
1 tablespoon chili-garlic sauce
2 teaspoons ground allspice

1. Put the beef, onion, garlic, miso, tomato paste, vinegar, brown sugar, ginger, mustard, chili-garlic sauce, and allspice in the slow cooker. Stir, then cover and cook on low for 8 to 10 hours.

2. Turn off the slow cooker. Divide the stew among serving bowls.

Per Serving: Calories: 286; Total Fat: 10g; Saturated Fat: 3g; Carbohydrates: 15g; Sodium: 931mg; Fiber: 2g; Protein: 35g

Chinese Beef Stew

DAIRY-FREE ● EGG-FREE ● NUT-FREE

Serves 6

Prep time: 5 minutes / Cook time: 8 to 10 hours

Chinese five-spice powder is a spice blend that includes cinnamon, cloves, fennel, star anise, and Sichuan peppercorns, although sometimes regular black pepper is used. It adds layers of complexity to this sweet and tangy beef stew, belying its simplicity. Serve it over steamed white rice.

2 pounds beef chuck, cut into 2-inch pieces

1 red onion, halved and thinly sliced from stem to roots

2 carrots, cut into ½-inch-thick slices

¼ cup minced garlic

2 tablespoons hoisin sauce

2 tablespoons low-sodium soy sauce

1 tablespoon minced fresh ginger

1 tablespoon rice-wine vinegar

2 teaspoons Chinese five-spice powder

½ teaspoon sea salt

4 cups Beef Stock (page 18) or store-bought

1. Put the beef, onion, carrots, garlic, hoisin, soy sauce, ginger, vinegar, five-spice powder, salt, and beef stock in the slow cooker. Stir, then cover and cook on low for 8 to 10 hours.

2. Turn off the slow cooker. Divide the stew among serving bowls.

✳ **Substitution Tip:** To make this dish gluten-free, use gluten-free hoisin and soy sauces.

Per Serving: Calories: 234; Total Fat: 9g; Saturated Fat: 2g; Carbohydrates: 7g; Sodium: 583mg; Fiber: 1g; Protein: 32g

Beef Bourguignon

DAIRY-FREE • EGG-FREE • NUT-FREE

Serves 6

Prep time: 20 minutes / Cook time: 8 to 10 hours

I learned to cook beef bourguignon while living in Europe and offered to prepare it for a visiting dignitary to the military base where my husband worked. Soon after, I learned that I would be cooking for 70 people and ordered 15 kilos of beef chuck from my local butcher. My kitchen looked like a slaughterhouse as I processed it all. With my friend Annette at my side, we seared every single piece of meat before adding it to the stew. It took forever. But eventually, every burner on my stove had a vat of stew simmering away, filling my kitchen with the aromas of red wine, herbs, and meat. The dinner was a smashing success except for one tiny detail—the guest of honor was vegetarian! Oh well. I'm letting you take the easy way out by using a brisket. It takes longer to cook but requires minimal prep.

¼ cup all-purpose flour

2 pounds beef brisket

Sea salt

Freshly ground black pepper

2 tablespoons canola oil, divided

2 cups dry red wine

4 carrots, cut into 2-inch pieces

8 ounces frozen pearl onions, thawed

8 ounces cremini mushrooms, sliced or whole

2 fresh thyme sprigs

1 fresh rosemary sprig

4 cups Beef Stock (page 18) or store-bought

1. Put the flour in a shallow dish.

2. Pat the beef with paper towels. Season liberally with salt and pepper, then dredge in the flour until it is lightly coated.

3. Heat a large skillet over medium-high heat.

4. Pour in a few teaspoons of oil, then add the beef. Sear on each side for about 5 minutes, or until well browned. Transfer to a medium bowl.

5. Pour the wine into the skillet. Using a wooden spoon, deglaze the skillet, scraping up the browned bits from the bottom. Simmer the wine for about 2 minutes to cook off some of the alcohol. Remove from the heat.

6. Put the carrots, onions, mushrooms, thyme, rosemary, and beef stock in the slow cooker. Top with the beef and any accumulated juices along with the wine. Stir, then cover and cook on low for 8 to 10 hours.

7. Turn off the slow cooker. Remove and discard the thyme and rosemary sprigs. Divide the stew among serving bowls.

❋ **Substitution Tip:** A gluten-free flour blend will work in place of the all-purpose flour. However, avoid using a single gluten-free flour (e.g., just brown rice flour or tapioca starch) because a blend of flours does a better job of replicating all-purpose flour.

Per Serving: Calories: 362; Total Fat: 13g; Saturated Fat: 3g; Carbohydrates: 13g; Sodium: 234mg; Fiber: 2g; Protein: 33g

MEASUREMENT CONVERSIONS

VOLUME EQUIVALENTS (LIQUID)

US Standard	US Standard (ounces)	Metric (approximate)
2 tablespoons	1 fl. oz.	30 mL
¼ cup	2 fl. oz.	60 mL
½ cup	4 fl. oz.	120 mL
1 cup	8 fl. oz.	240 mL
1½ cups	12 fl. oz.	355 mL
2 cups or 1 pint	16 fl. oz.	475 mL
4 cups or 1 quart	32 fl. oz.	1 L
1 gallon	128 fl. oz.	4 L

VOLUME EQUIVALENTS (DRY)

US Standard	Metric (approximate)
⅛ teaspoon	0.5 mL
¼ teaspoon	1 mL
½ teaspoon	2 mL
¾ teaspoon	4 mL
1 teaspoon	5 mL
1 tablespoon	15 mL
¼ cup	59 mL
⅓ cup	79 mL
½ cup	118 mL
⅔ cup	156 mL
¾ cup	177 mL
1 cup	235 mL
2 cups or 1 pint	475 mL
3 cups	700 mL
4 cups or 1 quart	1 L

OVEN TEMPERATURES

Fahrenheit (F)	Celsius (C) (approximate)
250°F	120°C
300°F	150°C
325°F	165°C
350°F	180°C
375°F	190°C
400°F	200°C
425°F	220°C
450°F	230°C

WEIGHT EQUIVALENTS

US Standard	Metric (approximate)
½ ounce	15 g
1 ounce	30 g
2 ounces	60 g
4 ounces	115 g
8 ounces	225 g
12 ounces	340 g
16 ounces or 1 pound	455 g

RESOURCES

Books

America's Test Kitchen, ed. *The Complete Slow Cooker: From Appetizers to Desserts—400 Must-Have Recipes That Cook While You Play (or Work).* Boston: America's Test Kitchen, 2017.

Ellgen, Pamela. *Healthy Slow Cooker Cookbook: 150 Fix-and-Forget Recipes Using Delicious, Whole-Food Ingredients.* Berkeley, CA: Rockridge Press, 2015.

Ellgen, Pamela. *Soup & Comfort: A Cookbook of Homemade Recipes to Warm the Soul.* Berkeley, CA: Arcas Publishing, 2015.

Given, Madeline. *The Anti-Inflammatory Diet Slow Cooker Cookbook: Prep-and-Go Recipes for Long-Term Healing.* Emeryville, CA: Rockridge Press, 2018.

Peterson, Karen Bellessa. *The Easy 5-Ingredient Slow Cooker Cookbook: 100 Delicious No-Fuss Meals for Busy People.* Berkeley, CA: Rockridge Press, 2017.

Websites

America's Test Kitchen: Best Slow Cookers
(AmericasTestKitchen.com/guides/healthy-slow-cooker/best-slow
-cookers-top-rated-brands-what-to-buy)

Crock-Pot Recipes
(Crock-Pot.com/recipes.html)

Surf Girl Eats
(SurfGirlEats.com)

The Kitchn: Slow Cooker
(thekitchn.com/collection/slow-cooker)

The Magical Slow Cooker
(TheMagicalSlowCooker.com)

REFERENCES

Bartoletti, Susan Campbell. "Soup Kitchen Act." In *Black Potatoes: The Story of the Great Irish Famine, 1845–1850*, 75. New York: Houghton Mifflin Harcourt, 2001.

Bramen, Lisa. "Count Rumford and the History of the Soup Kitchen." *Smithsonian Magazine*, December 29, 2010.

Charyn, Jerome. "The Shadow Behind Our Founding Fathers." *Washington Post*, June 22, 2008.

Mink, Gwendolyn, and Alice O'Connor, eds. "Food Banks." In *Poverty in the United States: An Encyclopedia of History, Politics, and Policy*, 321–23. Santa Barbara: ABC-CLIO, 2004.

Rumble, Victoria R. "Soup Kitchens." In *Soup Through the Ages: A Culinary History with Period Recipes*, 180–83. Jefferson, NC: McFarland & Company, 2009.

Squires, Nick. "Knights of Malta to Open Soup Kitchens in Britain." *Telegraph*. February 5, 2013.

Vernon, James. *Hunger: A Modern History*. Cambridge, MA: Harvard University Press, 2007.

Walter, Andrew. "Food Assistance Landscapes in the United States." In *Food and Famine in the 21st Century*, edited by William A. Dando, 171–80. Santa Barbara; ABC-CLIO, 2012.

Wetzsteon, Ross. *Republic of Dreams: Greenwich Village: The American Bohemia, 1910–1960*. New York: Simon and Schuster, 2003.

INDEX

A

Apricots, dried
    Moroccan Lamb
        Stew, 116
    Persian Lamb and
        Rice Soup, 80
Arroz Caldo, 72–73
Artichoke hearts
    Mediterranean Chicken
        Stew, 103
Avocados
    Cumin-Scented Chickpea
        and Tequila Soup, 55
    Polenta and Pork
        Stew, 113–114
    Simmered Pinto Beans
        with Avocado, 59
    Tender Pork Posole, 76–77
    Tres Chiles Grain Soup, 64
    White Chicken
        Chili, 88–89

B

Bacon. *See also* Pancetta
    Spinach and Apple
        Soup with Crumbled
        Bacon, 40–41
Barley
    Beef and Barley Soup, 81
    Tres Chiles Grain
        Soup, 64

Basil
    Chicken Pho, 74–75
    Creamy White Bean and
        Wheat Berry Stew, 101
    Miso and Kabocha
        Squash Soup, 52
    Panang Duck Curry with
        Pineapple, 111
    Tomato Soup, 26
Bean sprouts
    Chicken Pho, 74–75
Beans
    Beef Chuck Chili, 95
    Cannellini Bean and
        Cheddar Bisque, 38
    Chipotle and Black
        Bean Soup, 51
    Chipotle Turkey Chili, 92–93
    Creamy White Bean and
        Wheat Berry Stew, 101
    Ham and White Bean
        Stew, 112
    Minestrone, 45
    Pasta e Fagioli, 68
    Simmered Pinto Beans
        with Avocado, 59
    Three-Bean Vegan Chili, 86
    Tuscan Bread Soup, 46
    White Chicken Chili, 88–89
Beef
    Beef and Barley Soup, 81
    Beef Bourguignon, 120–121

    Beef Chuck Chili, 95
    Beef Stock, 18
    Chinese Beef Stew, 119
    Italian Wedding Soup, 79
    Miso Beef Stew, 118
Bok choy
    Wonton Broth, 22
Breads
    Buttermilk Corn Bread, 85
    Gruyère Crostini, 57
Broccoli Soup, Cream of, 36
Broths
    Chicken Broth, 17
    Essential Vegetable
        Broth, 14
    homemade vs.
        store-bought, 4
    Wonton Broth, 22
Buttermilk Corn Bread, 85

C

Cabbage
    Chicken Adobo Stew, 106
    Miso and Kabocha
        Squash Soup, 52
    Red Cabbage Slaw, 115
Cannellini Bean and
    Cheddar Bisque, 38
Carrot and Sweet Potato
    Soup, 28
Cauliflower Bisque, Creamy, 34

Cheese
  Beef Chuck Chili, 95
  Cannellini Bean and
    Cheddar Bisque, 38
  Creamy Cauliflower
    Bisque, 34
  Gruyère Crostini, 57
  Italian Wedding Soup, 79
  Pork Chili Verde, 94
  Sourdough Asiago
    Grilled Cheese, 27
  Spinach and Apple Soup with
    Crumbled Bacon, 40–41
  Tortilla Soup, 39
  Truffle-Mushroom
    Risotto Soup, 66
Chicken
  Arroz Caldo, 72–73
  Chicken Adobo Stew, 106
  Chicken Afritada Stew, 107
  Chicken and Corn
    Chowder, 84
  Chicken and Sausage
    Gumbo, 90–91
  Chicken Broth, 17
  Chicken Pho, 74–75
  Coconut-Curry Chicken
    Stew, 110
  Coq au Vin Blanc, 102
  Cuban Chicken Stew, 104
  Farro and Chicken Soup, 69
  Jamaican Jerk Chicken
    Stew, 108
  Mediterranean Chicken
    Stew, 103
  Miso and Kabocha
    Squash Soup, 52
  Polo en Escabeche, 105
  Sticky Rice and
    Ginger-Chicken
    Porridge, 70
  Tandoori Chicken
    Chowder, 87
  Tortilla Soup, 39
  White Chicken Chili, 88–89

Chickpeas
  Cumin-Scented Chickpea
    and Tequila Soup, 55
  Pork Chili Verde, 94
  Vibrant Chickpea
    Coconut Curry, 58
Chinese Beef Stew, 119
Chipotle and Black
  Bean Soup, 51
Chipotle Turkey Chili, 92–93
Chorizo and Wild Rice Soup, 71
Cilantro
  Beef Chuck Chili, 95
  Chicken Adobo Stew, 106
  Chicken Pho, 74–75
  Cumin-Scented Chickpea
    and Tequila Soup, 55
  Jamaican Jerk Chicken
    Stew, 108
  Persian Lamb and
    Rice Soup, 80
  Quinoa and Sweet
    Potato Soup, 63
  Red Cabbage Slaw, 115
  Sticky Rice and
    Ginger-Chicken
    Porridge, 70
  Tender Pork Posole, 76–77
  Tres Chiles Grain Soup, 64
  White Chicken Chili, 88–89
  Yellow Dal, 48
Clams
  Mediterranean Seafood
    Stew, 117
Coconut milk
  Coconut Curried
    Vegetable Soup, 47
  Coconut-Curry Chicken
    Stew, 110
  Creamy Wild Rice Soup, 65
  Panang Duck Curry with
    Pineapple, 111
  Thai Red Lentil Soup, 33
  Vibrant Chickpea
    Coconut Curry, 58

Collard Greens, Peanut
  Stew with, 100
Coq au Vin Blanc, 102
Corn
  Chicken and Corn
    Chowder, 84
  Quinoa and Sweet
    Potato Soup, 63
  Tortilla Soup, 39
Cream of Broccoli Soup, 36
Creamy Cauliflower Bisque, 34
Creamy Parsnip Bisque, 31
Creamy White Bean and
  Wheat Berry Stew, 101
Creamy Wild Rice Soup, 65
Cuban Chicken Stew, 104
Cumin-Scented Chickpea
  and Tequila Soup, 55

D

Dairy-free
  Arroz Caldo, 72–73
  Beef and Barley Soup, 81
  Beef Bourguignon, 120–121
  Beef Stock, 18
  Chicken Adobo Stew, 106
  Chicken Afritada Stew, 107
  Chicken Broth, 17
  Chicken Pho, 74–75
  Chinese Beef Stew, 119
  Chipotle and Black
    Bean Soup, 51
  Chipotle Turkey Chili, 92–93
  Chorizo and Wild
    Rice Soup, 71
  Coconut Curried
    Vegetable Soup, 47
  Coconut-Curry Chicken
    Stew, 110
  Cuban Chicken Stew, 104
  Cumin-Scented Chickpea
    and Tequila Soup, 55
  Dukkah, 29
  Essential Vegetable Broth, 14

Dairy-free (*continued*)

Farro and Chicken Soup, 69

Fennel and Farro Soup, 62

Fish Stock, 19

Ham and White Bean
Stew, 112

Herbed Bread Crumbs, 35

Jamaican Jerk Chicken
Stew, 108

Kale Salad, 67

Kombu Dashi, 16

Mediterranean Chicken
Stew, 103

Mediterranean Seafood
Stew, 117

Minestrone, 45

Miso and Kabocha
Squash Soup, 52

Miso Beef Stew, 118

Miso Soup, 21

Moroccan Lamb Stew, 116

Mushroom Stock, 15

Panang Duck Curry with
Pineapple, 111

Pasta e Fagioli, 68

Peanut Stew with Collard
Greens, 100

Persian Lamb and
Rice Soup, 80

Polenta and Pork
Stew, 113–114

Polo en Escabeche, 105

Quinoa and Sweet
Potato Soup, 63

Red Cabbage Slaw, 115

Roasted Red Pepper
Soup, 30

Simmered Pinto Beans
with Avocado, 59

Spicy Lentil Soup, 50

Split Pea Soup, 54

Sticky Rice and
Ginger-Chicken
Porridge, 70

Tender Pork Posole, 76–77

Thai Red Lentil Soup, 33

Three-Bean Vegan Chili, 86

Tomato Soup, 26

Tropical Fruit Salad, 109

Tuscan Bread Soup, 46

Vibrant Chickpea
Coconut Curry, 58

Wonton Broth, 22

Duck Curry with Pineapple,
Panang, 111

Dukkah, 29

E

Egg-free

Beef and Barley Soup, 81

Beef Bourguignon, 120–121

Beef Chuck Chili, 95

Beef Stock, 18

Cannellini Bean and
Cheddar Bisque, 38

Chicken Adobo Stew, 106

Chicken Afritada
Stew, 107

Chicken and Corn
Chowder, 84

Chicken and Sausage
Gumbo, 90–91

Chicken Broth, 17

Chicken Pho, 74–75

Chinese Beef Stew, 119

Chipotle and Black
Bean Soup, 51

Chipotle Turkey Chili, 92–93

Chorizo and Wild
Rice Soup, 71

Coconut Curried
Vegetable Soup, 47

Coconut-Curry Chicken
Stew, 110

Coq au Vin Blanc, 102

Cream of Broccoli Soup, 36

Creamy Cauliflower
Bisque, 34

Creamy Parsnip Bisque, 31

Creamy White Bean and
Wheat Berry Stew, 101

Creamy Wild Rice Soup, 65

Cuban Chicken Stew, 104

Cumin-Scented Chickpea
and Tequila Soup, 55

Dukkah, 29

Essential Vegetable Broth, 14

Farro and Chicken Soup, 69

Fennel and Farro Soup, 62

Fish Stock, 19

French Onion Soup, 56

Gruyère Crostini, 57

Ham and White Bean
Stew, 112

Hearty Cream of
Mushroom Soup, 32

Herbed Bread Crumbs, 35

Jamaican Jerk Chicken
Stew, 108

Kale Salad, 67

Kombu Dashi, 16

Mediterranean Chicken
Stew, 103

Mediterranean Seafood
Stew, 117

Minestrone, 45

Miso and Kabocha
Squash Soup, 52

Miso Beef Stew, 118

Miso Soup, 21

Moroccan Lamb Stew, 116

Mushroom Stock, 15

Panang Duck Curry with
Pineapple, 111

Pasta e Fagioli, 68

Peanut Stew with Collard
Greens, 100

Persian Lamb and
Rice Soup, 80

Polenta and Pork
Stew, 113–114

Polo en Escabeche, 105

Pork Chili Verde, 94

Potato-Leek Soup, 37

Quinoa and Sweet
    Potato Soup, 63
Red Cabbage Slaw, 115
Roasted Red Pepper
    Soup, 30
Seafood Chowder, 96
Simmered Pinto Beans
    with Avocado, 59
Sourdough Asiago
    Grilled Cheese, 27
Spicy Lentil Soup, 50
Spinach and Apple Soup with
    Crumbled Bacon, 40–41
Split Pea Soup, 54
Sticky Rice and
    Ginger-Chicken
    Porridge, 70
Sweet Potato and
    Carrot Soup, 28
Tadka, 49
Tandoori Chicken
    Chowder, 87
Tender Pork Posole, 76–77
Thai Red Lentil Soup, 33
Three-Bean Vegan Chili, 86
Tomato Soup, 26
Tortilla Soup, 39
Tres Chiles Grain Soup, 64
Tropical Fruit Salad, 109
Truffle-Mushroom
    Risotto Soup, 66
Tuscan Bread Soup, 46
Vibrant Chickpea
    Coconut Curry, 58
White Chicken Chili, 88–89
Wild Rice and Mushroom
    Soup, 53
Wonton Broth, 22
Yellow Dal, 48
Eggplants
    Mediterranean Seafood
    Stew, 117
Eggs
    Arroz Caldo, 72–73
    Italian Wedding Soup, 79

Endive
    Italian Wedding Soup, 79
Equipment, 2–3
Escarole
    Italian Wedding Soup, 79
Essential Vegetable Broth, 14

F

Farro
    Farro and Chicken Soup, 69
    Fennel and Farro Soup, 62
Fennel and Farro Soup, 62
Fish
    Fish Stock, 19
    Seafood Chowder, 96
French Onion Soup, 56

G

Gluten-free
    Arroz Caldo, 72–73
    Beef Chuck Chili, 95
    Beef Stock, 18
    Cannellini Bean and
        Cheddar Bisque, 38
    Chicken and Corn
        Chowder, 84
    Chicken Broth, 17
    Chicken Pho, 74–75
    Chipotle Turkey Chili, 92–93
    Chorizo and Wild
        Rice Soup, 71
    Coconut Curried
        Vegetable Soup, 47
    Coconut-Curry Chicken
        Stew, 110
    Coq au Vin Blanc, 102
    Cream of Broccoli Soup, 36
    Creamy Cauliflower
        Bisque, 34
    Creamy Parsnip Bisque, 31
    Creamy Wild Rice Soup, 65
    Cuban Chicken Stew, 104
    Dukkah, 29

Essential Vegetable Broth, 14
Fish Stock, 19
French Onion Soup, 56
Ham and White Bean
    Stew, 112
Hearty Cream of
    Mushroom Soup, 32
Jamaican Jerk Chicken
    Stew, 108
Kale Salad, 67
Kombu Dashi, 16
Mediterranean Chicken
    Stew, 103
Mediterranean Seafood
    Stew, 117
Miso and Kabocha
    Squash Soup, 52
Miso Soup, 21
Moroccan Lamb Stew, 116
Mushroom Stock, 15
Panang Duck Curry with
    Pineapple, 111
Persian Lamb and
    Rice Soup, 80
Polenta and Pork
    Stew, 113–114
Polo en Escabeche, 105
Pork Chili Verde, 94
Potato-Leek Soup, 37
Quinoa and Sweet
    Potato Soup, 63
Red Cabbage Slaw, 115
Roasted Red Pepper
    Soup, 30
Seafood Chowder, 96
Simmered Pinto Beans
    with Avocado, 59
Spicy Lentil Soup, 50
Spinach and Apple Soup with
    Crumbled Bacon, 40–41
Split Pea Soup, 54
Sticky Rice and
    Ginger-Chicken
    Porridge, 70
Sweet Potato and
    Carrot Soup, 28

Gluten-free (*continued*)
 Tadka, 49
 Tandoori Chicken
  Chowder, 87
 Tender Pork Posole, 76–77
 Thai Red Lentil Soup, 33
 Three-Bean Vegan Chili, 86
 Tomato Soup, 26
 Tortilla Soup, 39
 Tropical Fruit Salad, 109
 Truffle-Mushroom
  Risotto Soup, 66
 Vibrant Chickpea
  Coconut Curry, 58
 White Chicken Chili, 88–89
 Wild Rice and Mushroom
  Soup, 53
 Wonton Broth, 22
 Yellow Dal, 48
Green beans
 Chicken Adobo Stew, 106
 Coconut-Curry Chicken
  Stew, 110
 Panang Duck Curry with
  Pineapple, 111
Gruyère Crostini, 57

I

Italian Wedding Soup, 79

J

Jamaican Jerk Chicken
 Stew, 108

K

Kale
 Kale Salad, 67
 Tuscan Bread Soup, 46
Kombu Dashi, 16

L

Lamb
 Moroccan Lamb Stew, 116
 Persian Lamb and
  Rice Soup, 80
Leeks
 Chicken and Corn
  Chowder, 84
 Coq au Vin Blanc, 102
 Potato-Leek Soup, 37
Leftovers, 8
Lemongrass
 Chicken Pho, 74–75
Lentils
 Spicy Lentil Soup, 50
 Thai Red Lentil Soup, 33
 Yellow Dal, 48

M

Mangos
 Tropical Fruit Salad, 109
Mediterranean Chicken
 Stew, 103
Mediterranean Seafood
 Stew, 117
Melons
 Tropical Fruit Salad, 109

Minestrone, 45
Mint
 Chicken Pho, 74–75
 Chorizo and Wild
  Rice Soup, 71
 Creamy Wild Rice Soup, 65
 Persian Lamb and
  Rice Soup, 80
 Tandoori Chicken
  Chowder, 87
 Tropical Fruit Salad, 109
Miso
 Miso and Kabocha
  Squash Soup, 52
 Miso Beef Stew, 118
 Miso Soup, 21
 Wonton Broth, 22
Moroccan Lamb Stew, 116
Mushrooms
 Coq au Vin Blanc, 102
 Essential Vegetable Broth, 14
 Hearty Cream of
  Mushroom Soup, 32
 Mushroom Stock, 15
 Three-Bean Vegan Chili, 86
 Tres Chiles Grain Soup, 64
 Truffle-Mushroom
  Risotto Soup, 66
 Wild Rice and Mushroom
  Soup, 53
 Wonton Broth, 22
Mussels
 Seafood Chowder, 96

N

Noodles
 Chicken Pho, 74–75
Nut-free
 Arroz Caldo, 72–73
 Beef and Barley Soup, 81
 Beef Bourguignon, 120–121
 Beef Chuck Chili, 95
 Beef Stock, 18
 Buttermilk Corn Bread, 85

Ham
 Ham and White Bean
  Stew, 112
 Split Pea Soup, 54
Hearty Cream of Mushroom
 Soup, 32
Herbed Bread Crumbs, 35
Herbs, fresh. *See also specific*
 Ham and White Bean
  Stew, 112
 Mediterranean Seafood
  Stew, 117
 Tuscan Bread Soup, 46
Hominy
 Tender Pork Posole, 76–77

Cannellini Bean and
 Cheddar Bisque, 38
Chicken Adobo Stew, 106
Chicken Afritada Stew, 107
Chicken and Corn
 Chowder, 84
Chicken and Sausage
 Gumbo, 90–91
Chicken Broth, 17
Chicken Pho, 74–75
Chinese Beef Stew, 119
Chipotle and Black
 Bean Soup, 51
Chipotle Turkey Chili, 92–93
Chorizo and Wild
 Rice Soup, 71
Coq au Vin Blanc, 102
Cream of Broccoli Soup, 36
Creamy Cauliflower
 Bisque, 34
Creamy White Bean and
 Wheat Berry Stew, 101
Cuban Chicken Stew, 104
Cumin-Scented Chickpea
 and Tequila Soup, 55
Essential Vegetable Broth, 14
Farro and Chicken Soup, 69
Fennel and Farro Soup, 62
Fish Stock, 19
French Onion Soup, 56
Gruyère Crostini, 57
Ham and White Bean
 Stew, 112
Hearty Cream of
 Mushroom Soup, 32
Italian Wedding Soup, 79
Jamaican Jerk Chicken
 Stew, 108
Kale Salad, 67
Kombu Dashi, 16
Mediterranean Chicken
 Stew, 103
Mediterranean Seafood
 Stew, 117
Minestrone, 45

Miso and Kabocha
 Squash Soup, 52
Miso Beef Stew, 118
Miso Soup, 21
Mushroom Stock, 15
Pasta e Fagioli, 68
Persian Lamb and
 Rice Soup, 80
Polenta and Pork
 Stew, 113–114
Polo en Escabeche, 105
Pork Chili Verde, 94
Potato-Leek Soup, 37
Quinoa and Sweet
 Potato Soup, 63
Red Cabbage Slaw, 115
Roasted Red Pepper
 Soup, 30
Seafood Chowder, 96
Simmered Pinto Beans
 with Avocado, 59
Sourdough Asiago
 Grilled Cheese, 27
Spicy Lentil Soup, 50
Spinach and Apple Soup with
 Crumbled Bacon, 40–41
Split Pea Soup, 54
Sticky Rice and
 Ginger-Chicken
 Porridge, 70
Tadka, 49
Tandoori Chicken
 Chowder, 87
Tender Pork Posole, 76–77
Three-Bean Vegan Chili, 86
Tomato Soup, 26
Tortilla Soup, 39
Tres Chiles Grain Soup, 64
Tropical Fruit Salad, 109
Truffle-Mushroom
 Risotto Soup, 66
Tuscan Bread Soup, 46
White Chicken Chili, 88–89
Wild Rice and Mushroom
 Soup, 53

Wonton Broth, 22
Yellow Dal, 48
Nuts
 Dukkah, 29
 Herbed Bread Crumbs, 35
 Moroccan Lamb Stew, 116

O

Okra
 Chicken and Sausage
  Gumbo, 90–91
Olives
 Cuban Chicken Stew, 104
 Mediterranean Chicken
  Stew, 103
Onions
 Beef Bourguignon, 120–121
 French Onion Soup, 56
 Tadka, 49

P

Panang Duck Curry with
 Pineapple, 111
Pancetta
 Pasta e Fagioli, 68
Pantry staples, 5–6
Parsley
 Chicken and Sausage
  Gumbo, 90–91
 Chorizo and Wild
  Rice Soup, 71
 Creamy Cauliflower
  Bisque, 34
 Creamy White Bean and
  Wheat Berry Stew, 101
 Cuban Chicken Stew, 104
 Essential Vegetable Broth, 14
 Fish Stock, 19
 Minestrone, 45
 Pasta e Fagioli, 68
 Persian Lamb and
  Rice Soup, 80
 Seafood Chowder, 96

Parsley (*continued*)
Spicy Lentil Soup, 50
Spinach and Apple Soup with
Crumbled Bacon, 40–41
Wild Rice and Mushroom
Soup, 53
Parsnip Bisque, Creamy, 31
Pasta
Italian Wedding Soup, 79
Pasta e Fagioli, 68
Pasta e Fagioli, 68
Peanut Stew with Collard
Greens, 100
Peas
Cuban Chicken Stew, 104
Tandoori Chicken
Chowder, 87
Peppers
Beef Chuck Chili, 95
Chicken Afritada Stew, 107
Chicken and Sausage
Gumbo, 90–91
Chipotle and Black
Bean Soup, 51
Chipotle Turkey Chili, 92–93
Coconut-Curry Chicken
Stew, 110
Cuban Chicken Stew, 104
Cumin-Scented Chickpea
and Tequila Soup, 55
Essential Vegetable Broth, 14
Jamaican Jerk Chicken
Stew, 108
Mediterranean Chicken
Stew, 103
Panang Duck Curry with
Pineapple, 111
Polo en Escabeche, 105
Roasted Red Pepper
Soup, 30
Three-Bean Vegan Chili, 86
Tortilla Soup, 39
Tres Chiles Grain Soup, 64
White Chicken Chili, 88–89
Persian Lamb and Rice Soup, 80

Pineapple
Panang Duck Curry with
Pineapple, 111
Tropical Fruit Salad, 109
Polenta and Pork
Stew, 113–114
Polo en Escabeche, 105
Pork. *See also* Bacon; Ham;
Pancetta; Sausage
Cuban Chicken Stew, 104
Italian Wedding Soup, 79
Polenta and Pork
Stew, 113–114
Pork Chili Verde, 94
Tender Pork Posole, 76–77
Pork Chili Verde, 94
Potatoes
Beef and Barley Soup, 81
Chicken Afritada Stew, 107
Chicken and Corn
Chowder, 84
Creamy Cauliflower
Bisque, 34
Creamy Parsnip Bisque, 31
Potato-Leek Soup, 37
Seafood Chowder, 96
Spinach and Apple Soup with
Crumbled Bacon, 40–41
Tandoori Chicken
Chowder, 87
Potato-Leek Soup, 37

Q

Quinoa
Quinoa and Sweet
Potato Soup, 63
Quinoa and Sweet
Potato Soup, 63

R

Recipes, about, 10
Red Cabbage Slaw, 115
Reheating, 8

Rice
Arroz Caldo, 72–73
Chicken and Sausage
Gumbo, 90–91
Chorizo and Wild Rice Soup, 71
Coconut Curried
Vegetable Soup, 47
Creamy Wild Rice Soup, 65
Hearty Cream of
Mushroom Soup, 32
Persian Lamb and
Rice Soup, 80
Sticky Rice and
Ginger-Chicken Porridge, 70
Tres Chiles Grain Soup, 64
Wild Rice and Mushroom
Soup, 53
Roasted Red Pepper Soup, 30
Rosemary
Beef Bourguignon, 120–121
Chorizo and Wild
Rice Soup, 71
Herbed Bread Crumbs, 35
Pasta e Fagioli, 68
Truffle-Mushroom
Risotto Soup, 66
Wild Rice and Mushroom
Soup, 53

S

Salads
Kale Salad, 67
Red Cabbage Slaw, 115
Tropical Fruit Salad, 109
Salmon
Seafood Chowder, 96
Sandwiches
Sourdough Asiago
Grilled Cheese, 27
Sausage
Chicken and Sausage
Gumbo, 90–91
Chorizo and Wild
Rice Soup, 71

Scallops
  Seafood Chowder, 96
Seafood Chowder, 96
Shrimp
  Mediterranean Seafood
    Stew, 117
Simmered Pinto Beans
    with Avocado, 59
Soup kitchens, 9
Sourdough Asiago Grilled
    Cheese, 27
Spicy Lentil Soup, 50
Spinach
  Quinoa and Sweet
    Potato Soup, 63
  Spinach and Apple Soup with
    Crumbled Bacon, 40–41]
  Vibrant Chickpea
    Coconut Curry, 58
Spinach and Apple Soup with
    Crumbled Bacon, 40–41
Split peas
  Persian Lamb and
    Rice Soup, 80
  Split Pea Soup, 54
Squash. *See also* Zucchini
  Creamy Wild Rice Soup, 65
  Miso and Kabocha
    Squash Soup, 52
Sticky Rice and Ginger-Chicken
    Porridge, 70
Stocks
  Beef Stock, 18
  Fish Stock, 19
  Kombu Dashi, 16
  Mushroom Stock, 15
Storage, 8
Sweet potatoes
  Chipotle Turkey Chili, 92–93
  Coconut Curried
    Vegetable Soup, 47
  Quinoa and Sweet
    Potato Soup, 63
  Sweet Potato and
    Carrot Soup, 28

Tadka, 49
Tandoori Chicken Chowder, 87
Tender Pork Posole, 76–77
Thai Red Lentil Soup, 33
Three-Bean Vegan Chili, 86
Thyme
  Beef and Barley Soup, 81
  Beef Bourguignon, 120–121
  Cannellini Bean and
    Cheddar Bisque, 38
  Chicken and Corn
    Chowder, 84
  Chicken Broth, 17
  Coq au Vin Blanc, 102
  Creamy Cauliflower
    Bisque, 34
  Essential Vegetable Broth, 14
  Farro and Chicken Soup, 69
  French Onion Soup, 56
  Herbed Bread Crumbs, 35
  Minestrone, 45
  Mushroom Stock, 15
  Potato-Leek Soup, 37
  Seafood Chowder, 96
  Tomato Soup, 26
  Truffle-Mushroom
    Risotto Soup, 66
  Wild Rice and Mushroom
    Soup, 53
Tofu
  Miso Soup, 21
Tomatoes
  Beef Chuck Chili, 95
  Chicken and Sausage
    Gumbo, 90–91
  Chipotle Turkey Chili, 92–93
  Coconut-Curry Chicken
    Stew, 110
  Creamy White Bean and
    Wheat Berry Stew, 101
  Creamy Wild Rice Soup, 65
  Cumin-Scented Chickpea
    and Tequila Soup, 55

Mediterranean Chicken
    Stew, 103
Mediterranean Seafood
    Stew, 117
Minestrone, 45
Roasted Red Pepper
    Soup, 30
Simmered Pinto Beans
    with Avocado, 59
Three-Bean Vegan Chili, 86
Tomato Soup, 26
Tortilla Soup, 39
Tres Chiles Grain Soup, 64
Tuscan Bread Soup, 46
Tortilla Soup, 39
Tres Chiles Grain Soup, 64
Tropical Fruit Salad, 109
Troubleshooting, 7
Truffle-Mushroom
    Risotto Soup, 66
Turkey Chili, Chipotle, 92–93
Tuscan Bread Soup, 46

Vegan
  Chipotle and Black
    Bean Soup, 51
  Coconut Curried
    Vegetable Soup, 47
  Dukkah, 29
  Essential Vegetable Broth, 14
  Fennel and Farro Soup, 62
  Herbed Bread Crumbs, 35
  Kale Salad, 67
  Kombu Dashi, 16
  Minestrone, 45
  Miso Soup, 21
  Mushroom Stock, 15
  Peanut Stew with Collard
    Greens, 100
  Quinoa and Sweet
    Potato Soup, 63
  Red Cabbage Slaw, 115

Vegan (*continued*)
    Roasted Red Pepper
      Soup, 30
    Spicy Lentil Soup, 50
    Thai Red Lentil Soup, 33
    Three-Bean Vegan Chili, 86
    Tomato Soup, 26
    Tropical Fruit Salad, 109
    Tuscan Bread Soup, 46
Vegetarian. *See also* Vegan
    Buttermilk Corn Bread, 85
    Creamy Parsnip Bisque, 31
    Creamy White Bean and
      Wheat Berry Stew, 101
    Creamy Wild Rice Soup, 65
    Hearty Cream of
      Mushroom Soup, 32
    Sourdough Asiago
      Grilled Cheese, 27
    Sweet Potato and
      Carrot Soup, 28
    Tadka, 49

Tres Chiles Grain Soup, 64
Yellow Dal, 48
Vibrant Chickpea Coconut
    Curry, 58

W

Wheat berries
    Creamy White Bean and
      Wheat Berry Stew, 101
    Minestrone, 45
White Chicken Chili, 88–89
Wild Rice and Mushroom
    Soup, 53
Wonton Broth, 22

Y

Yellow Dal, 48
Yogurt
    Cream of Broccoli Soup, 36
    Creamy Parsnip Bisque, 31

Creamy Wild Rice Soup, 65
Sweet Potato and
    Carrot Soup, 28
Tandoori Chicken
    Chowder, 87

Z

Zucchini
    Coconut Curried
      Vegetable Soup, 47
    Mediterranean Seafood
      Stew, 117
    Tres Chiles Grain Soup, 64

ACKNOWLEDGMENTS

Thank you to my family for supporting me through another book, tasting recipes, sharing your honest feedback, and generally being awesome. I love you.

Thank you to my mom for instilling in me a love of home cooking and making meals with whole-food ingredients.

Thanks to the amazing team at Callisto who continually invite me into exciting projects, like this one, and shape the manuscripts into something far better than I could create on my own. Thanks especially to Rebecca Markley, Vanessa Putt, and Erika Sloan.

ABOUT THE AUTHOR

Pamela Ellgen is the author of more than a dozen cookbooks, including the bestselling *5-Ingredient College Cookbook*, *Soup & Comfort*, and *The Healthy Slow Cooker Cookbook*. Her work has been featured in *Outside* magazine, *TODAY Food*, *Healthline*, *HuffPost*, *Edible*, and *Darling Magazine*. She lives in Oceanside, California, with her husband and two sons and their goldendoodle, June. When she's not in the kitchen, she's surfing or sharing recipes at SurfGirlEats.com.

CPSIA information can be obtained
at www.ICGtesting.com
Printed in the USA
JSHW040034150720
6685JS00002B/15